RISE

———

HOW TO FIND YOUR PEOPLE, YOUR POWER AND PURPOSE IN YOUR JOURNEY TOWARDS SUCCESS

CHARITY MAJORS   ELIZABETH SCARCELLA

HEATHER MCNALLY   HEATHER OLSON

MARY SEMENZA   MELANIE HERSCHORN

NOELLE KUSTAS

ARISE
PUBLISHING HOUSE

RISE
How to Find Your People, Your Power and Purpose in Your Journey
Towards Success

Published by ARISE Publishing House
Boise, Idaho, U.S.A

QUANTITY PURCHASES: Companies, professional groups,
schools, clubs, and other organizations may qualify for special terms
when ordering quantities of this title.

For information, email charity@charitymajors.com.

Thank you for getting "RISE"

CONTENTS

INTRODUCTION

CHARITY MAJORS

In a world that measures success by titles, trophies, and how quickly you climb the ladder, the word **"Rise"** might sound like another call to hustle harder, push further, and never show weakness. But this book—*Rise: How to Find Your People, Power, and Purpose in Your Journey Towards Success*—is not about that kind of rise.

This is about a different kind of ascent.

Imagine yourself standing in that stillness just before dawn. The air is cool and heavy, the world wrapped in silence. Maybe you're cocooned in a blanket, feeling its rough edges, listening to your own breath and the hush pressing in from every side. The darkness feels endless—thick enough to swallow hope whole. Maybe you know that darkness: the kind that settles deep in your bones when life doesn't go as planned, when the dreams of your heart seem so distant you wonder if they were ever real.

You look out and see nothing but shadow. You feel the ache of longing, the sting of disappointment, the weight of wondering if you'll ever be enough. Maybe you've been told to quiet your voice, to shrink yourself to fit in, to stop dreaming so big. Maybe you've felt the cold sting of betrayal, the emptiness of broken promises, or the hunger that comes from growing up with less than you needed and more than you could bear.

But then—almost before you realize it—the sky begins to change. A soft blush of pink and gold creeps along the horizon, painting the clouds with light. You feel the first warm touch of sunlight on your face. You hear a bird's song, hesitant at first, then growing stronger, as if it knows the sun is coming. The world begins to stir: the scent of dew on grass, the distant hum of life waking up, the fresh taste of hope in the air.

This is the rise we are talking about.

The rise that happens in the quiet moments, before the world wakes up and the sun breaks through the darkness.

The rise where light breaks through the darkness and expands to touch everything around it. Not the race to the top, but the courage to stand up, again and again, even when your knees are bruised and your heart is tired.

The rise that happens when you hold onto the dreams that live deep in your heart, even when nothing in your world seems to match them.

The rise that begins when you dare to believe in more—more for yourself, more for your family, more for the world—when every sign tells you to settle for less.

But rising isn't something we do alone. It's not just about finding your footing; it's about finding your people. The women whose stories fill these pages have discovered that the journey toward success is not a solitary climb. It's about reaching out, finding those who see your light, who encourage you to keep going, who remind you of your worth when you've forgotten it yourself. Sometimes your people are found in laughter over coffee, in tears spilled during late-night calls, in the quiet understanding that comes from shared struggle. True connection isn't about fitting in—it's about being seen: messy, real, and unfiltered. When we find our people, we find the courage to be ourselves, to speak our truth, and to rise higher than we ever could alone.

As you journey through *Rise: How to Find Your People, Power, and Purpose in Your Journey Towards Success*, you'll see that finding your people is only the beginning. The stories here reveal how, in the company of others, we discover our own power. Not the kind of power that dominates or controls, but the kind that comes from presence. The power to stand tall in your truth, to own your story, to use your voice—even when it shakes. Power is knowing you are enough, just as you are. It's the fire in your belly that refuses to be extinguished, the resilience that keeps you moving forward, the light that shines from within and illuminates the way for others.

And as you rise, as you find your people and your power, you begin to uncover your purpose. Purpose isn't always a lightning bolt or a grand calling. Sometimes, it's a quiet knowing that grows with every step you take. It's the spark that lights your soul when you help someone else, the satisfaction you feel when you use your gifts, the deep rightness that comes from living in alignment with your values. For some, purpose is born from pain—from lessons learned in hardship, from the desire to make sure others don't walk the same lonely roads. Each woman in this book found her purpose not by following someone else's path, but by listening to her own heart, honoring her own story, and trusting that her journey had meaning—even when the map was unclear.

But there is something even deeper at play here—something that connects us all, no matter where we come from or what we've endured: the power of our stories.

Stories are more than words on a page. They are bridges—building bonds between hearts across distances and generations. They are mirrors—reflecting our hidden fears, secret hopes, and wildest dreams.

Stories remind us we are not alone in our struggles, that our pain and joy are shared, that our journeys matter.

And stories are sacred. Since the dawn of time, stories have been the golden thread that weaves humanity together—carried around campfires, whispered in the dark, written in journals, and passed from one heart to another. They are the soul's song, the heartbeat of history, the map that guides us home to ourselves and to each other. When we honor our stories—both the ones we live and the ones we share— we honor the legacy of every woman who has ever dared to rise.

The stories in this book are not roadmaps for shortcuts or formulas for success. They are permission slips —inviting you to be real, vulnerable, and to own every piece of your journey. They are here to remind you that *your* story is powerful and worthy of being told. When we share our stories, we give others permission to do the same. We create space for healing, understanding, and transformation.

There is magic in being seen and heard. When we meet each other authentically, when we drop the masks and show up in our humanness, we create alchemy. Our scars become survival guides, our victories inspire hope, and our voices—no matter how shaky —spark revolutions within ourselves and others.

So, before you turn the page, I invite you to pause and make some sacred agreements with yourself as you move through these stories. These are not rules, but reminders—soulful signposts to guide you as you read, reflect, and rise. Let them be your compass as you navigate the valleys of vulnerability and the peaks of possibility, as you cross the bridges of bravery and the rivers of resilience:

- **Keep your heart open.** Allow these stories to stir your spirit, challenge your perspectives, and awaken empathy for yourself and others.

- **Honor your own journey.** Resist the urge to compare or diminish your story. Every path has purpose; every scar holds significance.

- **Promise not to play small.** When you feel the urge to shrink, to silence your voice, or to settle for less, remember: you are meant for more.

- **Persevere when it gets hard.** When a story hits close to home, when emotions bubble up, when you want to close the book—stay. Sit with the discomfort. Let it teach you, stretch you, strengthen you.

- **Seek your people.** Notice the names, faces, and voices that echo your own. Reach out, connect, and remember: community creates courage.

- **Protect your power.** When you feel your light dimming, pause. Breathe. Reclaim your brilliance and let it shine, even if only for yourself.

- **Pursue your purpose.** Let every lesson, every moment of meaning, move you closer to the life you long for.

Let this be your season of rising:
  A season of courage over comfort,
  connection over comparison,

and compassion over criticism.

May you find, in these pages, not just stories, but soul-deep reminders that your voice matters, your dreams deserve daylight, you were made to shine, and your rise is already underway.

Because when one of us rises, we all rise.

I rise, you rise.

Together, we rise—brighter, bolder, beautifully unbreakable.

To the girl I used to be—
from a small town, with big dreams.
For breaking free, finding your own way,
and building a life full of love, strength, and purpose.
To my husband and our three beautiful children—
you are my greatest adventure.

— Mary Semenza

ONE
FROM SMALL TOWN TO BIG DREAMS

MARY SEMENZA

When I was a little girl, I was told that big dreams weren't meant for people like me. "You're from a small town; people like us don't go far," they said. But I never let those words take root in my heart.

THE WORDS only fueled my desire to prove that the world is not bound by geography or circumstance. I learned that my dreams weren't limited by the place I was born or the struggles I faced — they were bound only by the limits I placed on myself.

Growing up in a small town, surrounded by limitations and doubts, I could have easily believed that my dreams were too big, too bold, or too impossible. But I refused to let the noise around me define my potential.

As far back as I can remember, I had visions of a

beautiful life: a loving family, a gorgeous home, and adventures around the world. I didn't know how or when, but I knew that God had planted those seeds in my heart. There were moments when the future seemed uncertain, when doubt would creep in, but I always held on to the dream that something bigger awaited me.

I knew that small-town mentality wasn't going to allow me to succeed in life. What I didn't know, though, was that the small-town mindset isn't just geographical—it's internal. It's something you can carry with you without even realizing it, because you don't know what you don't know.

As I began my journey into adulthood, I quickly learned that my struggles with money were far from over. Yes, I was finally earning my very own paycheck. But I had no idea how to manage it. Where I come from, when someone gets money, the first instinct is to spend it. Saving, budgeting, and planning ahead weren't things we ever talked about.

I was working and attending college, doing every-thing I thought I was supposed to do—but I didn't have extra money. Someone suggested I take out student loans, and without really understanding the long-term consequences, I did. That's a decision I'm still paying for today.

And then, I got pregnant. The pregnancy was diffi-cult, and I became so sick that I had to drop out of school. One obstacle after another began to pile up, and for the first time, I started to doubt myself. I held onto the belief that I could still reach my goals, but the path ahead was foggy at best.

I kept pushing forward, even when it seemed like the odds were against me. There were days when I felt isolated, wondering if I would ever get to experience the life I dreamed of. But there were also moments of undeniable clarity, moments when the future seemed just within reach. I would daydream of traveling, meeting new people, and building a future I could be proud of.

And then, something miraculous happened. Those visions began to manifest into reality. It wasn't instantaneous; it took years of hard work, persistence, and faith. Slowly, I started to see glimpses of the life I had always dreamed of.

> Each step I took, every goal I set, brought me closer to where I am today. It wasn't about waiting for the perfect moment — it was about making every moment count.

Today, I'm living proof that no matter where you come from or what limitations you face, your dreams are possible. It's not always easy, but it's worth it. And I want to remind you that if I could do it, so can you. Keep moving forward, trust in your vision, and watch as the life you've always wanted begins to unfold. Your dreams aren't just for a lucky few — they are for anyone willing to work for them.

The Heart of a Giver

Growing up in a small town, raised by a single mother, meant living with constant uncertainty. We often went without basic necessities—there were times when the lights were off, the heat didn't work, and food was scarce. Birthdays and holidays passed quietly, without presents or celebration, just the weight of trying to get through another day. I could have easily adopted a mindset of scarcity and selfishness. But instead, my childhood experiences instilled in me a deep-seated desire to give. Despite everything we didn't have, my mom always taught me that generosity isn't about what you have; it's about the heart you have.

My husband often asks me where this trait comes from, and I believe it's rooted in my upbringing. My mom, a single parent, was a giver despite our limited means. She would always find a way to help others, even when we didn't have much ourselves. I recall one Christmas when we were struggling financially. Our family barely had enough for our own gifts, but my mom still found a way to give to a family in need. It was a small gesture, but the impact it had on me was enormous. I remember asking her how she could do that when we didn't have enough for ourselves, and she simply said, "Because love isn't measured by what you have, it's measured by what you're willing to share."

Her selflessness wasn't a one-time thing. It was a consistent theme throughout my childhood. Whether it was volunteering her time at the local church or making sure no one in our neighborhood went without, my mom's heart was always open. She showed me that giving isn't about quantity; it's about the quality of the love and intention behind the act.

As I've grown, I've carried that same spirit of generosity into my adult life. It's something I instill in my children, teaching them that the greatest joy comes not from what we receive, but from what we give. Every day, I try to model kindness and selflessness, believing that the more we give, the more we make space in our hearts for greater blessings. My giving isn't always in material form; sometimes it's offering a listening ear, a kind word, or support in times of need.

Even when we don't have much to give, we always have something to share — whether it's love, kindness, or encouragement. This is a lesson I carry with me every day: to approach life with a giving heart, knowing that the more we give, the richer our lives become.

Overcoming Adversity

At one point, it felt like every weight life could throw was stacked on my shoulders. I was a young, first-time mother, trying to figure out what motherhood even looked like, while still trying to figure out who I was. I had suddenly traded the energetic, lively music and distinct aroma of sweat and perfumes you get in a nightclub, for the sounds of a crying baby and the smells of vomit and dirty diapers. I was working just to keep up with bills and childcare costs, which created more challenges, especially since I often got off work after daycare had already closed for the day. I was constantly scrambling, always behind.

At the same time, I was still young and trying to hold onto the pieces of my life that reminded me I was more than just a mother. I tried to balance the realities of parenthood with the desire to maintain friendships and have a social life, but that balancing act was exhausting. And as I grew, I began to realize that some of the relationships I had clung to weren't healthy for me anymore. Letting go of those relationships was painful, but necessary. I was starting to understand that growth sometimes means walking away, even when it hurts.

There were nights when I didn't know how I was going to make it through the next day. The memories of my childhood began to engulf my thoughts. I could not only picture myself sitting in a cold house, with no heat or lights, but my bones would physically ache, my skin would get cold, and internally, it was as if I had been consumed with the cold of night. I would sometimes feel that sadness that only a disappointed child with no presents to open on Christmas understands.

But through it all, I learned to trust myself, to

trust my instincts, and to trust the vision that
God had given me for my life.

There were days when I felt like the odds were
stacked against me, but I learned that it's often in those
darkest moments that we find our greatest strength.
There's a saying I often remind myself of, which was
originally written in the 1600s by an English theolo-
gian: "The darkest hour is just before the dawn." And
it's true. Just when I thought I couldn't go any further,
a light would appear, whether in the form of a kind
word from a stranger, an unexpected opportunity, or a
moment of clarity.

One evening, sitting in my car in the parking lot, I
felt completely overwhelmed. I had just finished a long
day of work, and the weight of my responsibilities felt
suffocating. I closed my eyes and said a prayer, asking
for strength and guidance. In that moment of silence, I
felt a profound peace wash over me. I didn't have all
the answers, but I knew I wasn't alone. From that
moment, I made a promise to myself that I would keep
going, no matter how hard it got.

I want to inspire people to hold onto their dreams,
to believe in themselves, and to never give up. No
matter how hard things get, the struggles you face
today are just stepping stones to the person you are
becoming.

Living a Life of Purpose and Service

The act of service isn't just something I do; it's a way of life.

My morning routine sets the tone for my day. I wake up at 2:30 a.m., head to the gym by 3 a.m., and then meditate, read my Bible, and pray. This quiet time helps me center myself and connect with my purpose. It's my sacred space where I gather strength for the day ahead. And it's in these quiet moments that I often hear God's voice, guiding me on what I need to do next.

Journaling is also an essential part of my daily routine. It allows me to reflect on my thoughts, feelings, and experiences. By putting my thoughts on paper, I'm able to process and release them, making space for new insights and growth. There's something powerful about writing – it helps me clarify my intentions and stay grounded in my purpose.

Living a healthy lifestyle is crucial to me. I believe that taking care of our physical, mental, and spiritual health is essential to living a life of purpose. When we feel good, we're more capable of serving others and making a positive impact in the world. A healthy body, a strong mind, and a centered spirit allow me to be the best version of myself for those around me.

Having a healthy mindset is the foundation of achieving our goals and living our best lives. It's not just about empowering others; it's about empowering ourselves first. When we believe in ourselves, we're unstoppable. We are capable of achieving great things, and by helping others along the way, we create a ripple effect that can change the world.

I want to inspire others to adopt a growth mindset, to believe in themselves, and to never give up on their dreams. By sharing my story, I hope to show that anyone can overcome obstacles, achieve their goals, and live a life of purpose and service.

Your Story Matters

Your struggles, your triumphs, your dreams – they all matter. Don't let anyone or anything make you feel like your story is too small, too insignificant, or too ordinary. Your story is unique, and it has the power to inspire and uplift others.

I used to think that my story wasn't important, that no one would care about the struggles I faced. But as I've opened up and shared more of my journey, I've realized that it's in our vulnerability that we connect with others. People don't want to hear about perfection. They want to hear about real life–about the messy moments, the highs and lows, the victories and defeats.

Now I have a challenge for you. It's time for you to own your story, to share your story, and to never apologize for who you are and what you've been through. Your experiences are what make you strong. They shape your perspective and give you a voice.

You are strong, capable, and resilient. And your story is a testament to that strength. Don't keep it to yourself. Share it with the world. You never know who you might inspire or uplift by doing so.

Remember that no matter what challenges you face, you are never alone.

Every step you take toward your dreams, no matter how small, brings you closer to the person you are meant to become. Keep pushing forward. Your story is just beginning.

ABOUT THE AUTHOR: MARY SEMENZA

Mary Semenza

Mary Semenza is a motivator at heart, a passionate entrepreneur, and a true girls' girl who believes deeply in the power of women uplifting one another. With 18 years of experience in the dental industry, Mary spent her career helping others succeed—until she finally decided it was time to bet on herself.

Fueled by a lifelong dream and a love for fashion

and empowerment, she launched **Grace and Clark Boutique**, an online destination that celebrates confidence, self-expression, and inclusion for all women, of all shapes and sizes.

Mary's journey from employee to business owner was rooted in her desire to inspire others—to show women what's possible when they believe in themselves. She's passionate about helping others grow, find their voice, and chase their dreams. Whether through fashion, mentorship, or her writing, she's dedicated to pouring into her community and making every woman feel seen, supported, and unstoppable.

In everything she does, Mary leads with heart. She's committed to creating spaces—both online and offline—where women feel empowered, beautiful, and encouraged to become the best version of themselves.

Her excerpt in this book is a reflection of that mission: to motivate, uplift, and remind readers that it's never too late to rewrite your story—and make it one you truly love.

Learn more: https://linktr.ee/marysemenza

Dedication

———

To God, the Ultimate Healer. And to every high-achieving woman who has carried the weight of the world, may you finally come to know the peace, clarity, and healing that were always meant for you.

— Elizabeth Grace Scarcella

TWO

SHATTERING THE SILENCE: SPEAKING UP IN A WORLD THAT PREFERRED ME VOICELESS

ELIZABETH SCARCELLA

The glass exploded before I even registered the sound. Metal slammed metal. My body jolted, then folded, and then vanished into black.

I WAS on the road again, Miami to Orlando, racking up another few hundred miles for a job that had me living inside a car. As the youngest Human Resources Director in a multi-state convenience store chain, I logged nearly 100,000 miles a year, all within the state of Florida.

My office wasn't a building. It was a front seat, a seatbelt, and a phone on silent. Lunches were protein bars from the stores I served, choked down between site visits and damage control.

Yes, a convenience store chain, which was almost

comical, considering I've never liked pumping my own gas. It's dirty. Smelly. Vaguely primal. I was all about high heels and blowouts in a world of oil-stained uniforms and windshield squeegees.

I didn't fit in. I never had. But I tried.

I learned to play by their rules. Smiled when they stared. Softened when they challenged. My job wasn't to manage stores; it was to manage the mess behind them. Sexual harassment complaints. Staffing crises. Workplace abuse.

Ironically, I was there to protect others from the very kinds of violations I'd later endure. And still, I showed up in full glam to a world that barely looked up.

Posture high. Lipstick intact. Hoping that would be enough.

It wasn't. Still, I did what I always did. I made it work. Or at least, I tried to. Until the moment I couldn't.

The Aftermath

On an ordinary May afternoon, everything changed. One moment, I was in control. The next, I was shattered.

It wasn't just the glass. The crash fractured my face. Rattled my brain.

Compressed my cervical spine. Collapsed my pelvic floor. Paralyzed my dominant hand.

My nervous system lit up like a downed power

line. I couldn't sleep. Couldn't think. Could barely speak, forgetting even the most basic words. And still, no one told me what had happened. I don't think they knew. The UPS driver who careened into me never even stopped.

I woke up in a forgotten outpost. The kind of backroad medical facility with flickering fluorescent lights, no clear signage, and definitely no trauma team.

Not a full-service hospital. Not even a decent ER. Just a place that felt like a rough draft of what medical care should be.

I was placed on a hard, unforgiving board and left alone...waiting for someone, anyone, to tell me what the CT scan had found. But no one came. Worse, no one even seemed to know where I was. My cell phone had been lost in the wreckage, along with any way to reach out, or be reached.

It wasn't just the pain that gripped me. It was the realization that I was invisible. Alone.

The longer I waited, the louder the truth became: I hadn't just been injured. I'd been dropped. Not just from a car, but from everything I thought would catch me.

And interestingly, this wasn't just any Monday in May. It was Cinco de Mayo, a holiday commemorating resistance and independence. But for me, it marked the beginning of the most brutal fight of my life. Not just to recover, but to reclaim. Because what followed wasn't healing. It was war.

A New Fight

Discharge didn't mean I was okay; it meant I was dropped into a maze with no map. No follow-ups. No plan. No coordinated care. I wasn't walking out of a facility. I was stepping into a battlefield.

Recovery consumed the next two years. Five days a week. Every week. Physical therapists stretched what was left. Chiropractors tried to realign what the crash had shattered. Neurologists. Orthopedists. Physiatrists. All speaking in scans and codes. Very few looked up long enough to see the woman inside the wreckage.

I tried everything: biofeedback. Acupuncture. Massage. And the needles. I hated them. But by then, my fear didn't matter. They became as routine as brushing my teeth. This wasn't a wellness journey. It was agony in sterile disguise. Each session stripped me down, so I could be rebuilt, one trembling muscle at a time.

There were surgeries. Words I had to relearn. Nights without sleep. My body unraveled faster than I could catch it. My wrist, my dominant hand, limp and lifeless. My pelvic floor collapsed. My dignity followed. My hair thinned in clumps. My teeth loosened until braces were the only thing holding them in.

I didn't recognize the reflection staring back at me.

Not a woman. Not yet. Just a shadow held together by medical tape and sheer will.

A Deeper Ache

And still, under all that? There was something deeper. A quieter ache that didn't begin with the crash, but had already rooted itself in my childhood.

Long before I was broken on impact, I had already learned what it felt like to be left. To be overshadowed by things more urgent than me. To watch love go missing, and wonder if it was something I did. To realize that sometimes, the people who should protect you... don't.

I was left to make sense of things far too big for any child to carry. So I became the girl who didn't need too much. The one who figured it out. The one who held it together. But when my body finally gave out, so did the old ways of coping. What broke wasn't just my bones; it was my belief that survival was the same thing as being okay.

A Traumatic Twist

Months into my recovery, while I was still relearning how to move, how to speak, how to be in my own body, I was drugged with GHB and left unconscious in the backseat of a locked car by a man I had trusted. I had been dating him for months. I had traveled with him.

Met his parents. Even spent time with his son, a child he rarely saw, and even more rarely mentioned. That should have been a sign. If he couldn't care for his own child, what made me believe he'd care for me?

The night began like so many others. He made me a drink before we went out. A vodka tonic. I took a sip and paused. "This tastes weird," I said. "Kind of like baking soda." He brushed it off, grinning. "You're imagining things."

I wasn't. I felt it hit me in the car. Woozy. Detached. Like I was watching my own body from somewhere far away. I remember walking into a nightclub. Lights. Music. Heat. And then...black.

I never made it through the night.

He carried me back to the car, my body limp and unresponsive, and dropped me into the passenger seat like I was nothing. I came to, just barely, and breathlessly whispered, "What's happening?" But there was no concern. Only blame. He said I wasn't acting right in the bar...as if I had done this to myself. Then he shut the door, locked it, and left me there. Alone. Disoriented. Trapped.

And just like that, I was invisible again.

While he went back inside to party with another woman, I lay there, discarded in the same kind of silence I'd known in that hospital hallway. No explanation. No comfort. Just another car. Another kind of shattering. Another moment where I disappeared, piece by piece, and no one noticed.

And I would've stayed there; alone, unconscious, and covered in vomit, if not for a sheriff who happened to walk by. By sheer coincidence, he recognized the car. Recognized me. And when he looked inside, something must've told him the truth. He shattered the windshield to pull me out.

And as the man who had left me came walking back toward the car... laughing, carefree, unaware, the sheriff had just pulled me out. He arrested him on the spot.

What I'd ingested could've killed me. GHB is often called the "date rape drug", tasteless to some, barely bitter to others. It slows the heart rate, blurs memory, and erases consent. It's colorless. Odorless. And almost always administered in silence. Like betrayal with a half-smile.

That night didn't just fracture something. It confirmed what had already been broken: my sense of safety, my ability to trust, and the belief that love would show up for me when it mattered most.

So while I was fighting to rebuild what medicine couldn't fully repair–my bones, my brain, my balance– I was also carrying something far heavier: a violation no scan could detect. A betrayal that nearly cost me my life.

Another Great Betrayal

Somehow, through all of this, I still had a job. This rebuilding was taking place while I was still reporting to a boss who mocked my pain, inside a system that punished honesty, trying to hold together a life that had been splintered in every possible way.

I was learning how to live inside a body that no longer felt like home, gathering pieces that didn't quite fit, tracing outlines of the woman I used to be.

The mirror was honest. Not cruel, just clear. It reflected someone I hadn't yet learned to recognize. Not only because I was broken, but because I had been quiet for too long. And in that silence, I began to hear the faintest sound of something returning: Not the woman I currently was, but the woman who was still in there. Still listening. Still rising.

And that boss? He made sure I knew just how inconvenient my pain really was. The mockery wasn't occasional. It was constant. Eye rolls when I handed in doctors' notes. Scoffs when I explained treatment plans. Snide remarks about my practitioners, as though healing was some kind of punchline.

"Quackery," he'd say with a smirk. Like trusting your body was foolish. Anything outside their system, didn't count. I didn't know it yet, but that word would find me again.

It wasn't just the words that wore me down. It was the culture that bred them. A system in which cruelty passed for leadership and silence kept you safe.

No place was that more obvious than on Fridays. There were no emails. No calendar invites. Just a quiet, shared understanding: if you didn't go, you weren't in. And if you weren't in, you weren't protected.

At first, it seemed harmless enough, just a tradition. A standing breakfast at a greasy diner with my boss and the older sales director. Same booth. Same waitress. They knew her name. She didn't know theirs.

I didn't eat bacon. I didn't eat eggs. I was already gluten-free. But I wasn't about to ask for fruit and cottage cheese...not in that world. Because in that world, asking for anything different marked you as difficult. And fitting in wasn't a strategy. It was survival.

Then came the drive. Always in his car. Always a flex. The passenger seat was never offered; it was expected. He had the title. The seniority. The keys. And with one hand on the wheel, he set the course. The stated plan never changed:

"We're just going to check on a few stores." But we all knew better.

The numbers were online. The reports came in every morning. No store visit was ever needed, and certainly not on a Friday. Still, I got into that passenger seat each time. Because not getting in had its own consequences.

That car had already become a kind of coffin, where pieces of me quietly disappeared. I'd nearly died in one car. Been drugged in another. And now, here I was...again in the passenger seat...watching my soul erode one unspoken mile at a time.

There was never an announcement. No heads-up. No ask. He would just turn the wheel, casually, like any other turn, and suddenly, we were pulling into a strip club parking lot before noon. Like it was normal. Like it was part of the route.

Inside, I would order a drink I didn't want. I rarely drank. But I needed to dull something. My stomach churned while they slid bills into dancers' G-strings.

My boss would hand me a dollar, half-laughing, half-daring, and ask if I wanted to "get in on the fun." I smiled. I laughed. I played the cool girl who could hang.

But inside? I was unraveling.

I didn't believe those women wanted to be there. I believed they were stuck, like me, caught in a loop they didn't choose, paid just enough to play along, but never quite enough to leave. And there I was: a woman helping to exploit other women, just to keep my seat at the table.

I felt sick. Sexually. Emotionally. Ethically. Spiritually. But I stayed. Because some part of me still believed that staying was safer than leaving. Even when the seatbelt had long since become a shackle.

Afterward, it still wasn't over. Most of the time, we'd end up at a smoky, windowless bar; the kind of place that felt like a funeral for something you couldn't quite name. We'd sit long enough for me to call a friend for a ride, like a teenager who'd stayed too long at a party she never wanted to attend.

The whole day felt like theater. A performance I couldn't stop repeating because the only thing scarier than being there was being left out. What I craved wasn't the drink. Or the dollar bill. Or the nod from men who barely saw me. What I craved was belonging. To be recognized. To be chosen. To be seen as someone worth protecting. To matter in a room where I was mostly invisible.

The Turning Point

Then came the moment I should've known was a warning, a foreshadowing. The kind of line that only sounds like prophecy when it's in the rearview mirror: he had found out I'd been attending personal development workshops, that I was trying to reclaim more than just my health. Something in him shifted.

He followed me outside to my car. His shadow longer than mine in the afternoon sun. Cigarette smoldering between two fingers. Voice low, edged in condescension.

"If you think you're so great," he muttered, "then go get another job."

He didn't know I was in therapy. I'd only told one person. Someone I thought I could trust. But in that office, healing was treated like delusion, something to mock, minimize, or ignore. Even recovery had to ride in the trunk. Tucked away. Out of sight.

That place didn't just demand silence. It punished truth.

A few weeks later, I was called into his office. No explanation. No lead-in. Just one last summons. There was no eye contact. No compassion. Just a single sentence, delivered like a software update:

"We're letting you go."

This time, what broke wasn't my body; it was the hope that I had a place, even in a world that only wanted pieces of me. Because somehow, that moment, that clean, clinical cut, hit harder than the crash. Harder than the sexual harassment. Harder than being drugged and left behind.

Because through it all, the disfigured body, the long recovery, the private shame, I'd still held on to one thread: my paycheck. And that paycheck meant survival. It meant my mortgage. It meant access to care. It meant keeping the company car I used for everything–therapy, appointments, groceries.

That car had once symbolized mobility. But now, it was proof I was only allowed to go where they let me. Technically, it was for business use only. Mileage tracked. Personal use discouraged.

But in that culture, the real rule was unspoken:
Drive where you're told or be left behind.

The only true policy was silence. Don't speak. Don't challenge. Don't disrupt. So, I played it safe. I stayed in my lane. I rode in silence, which is why it gutted me when I was the only one laid off. Out of thousands of employees, across 140 stores and an entire executive tier, just me. No transition. No warning. No one even pretending to take my place.

I had been the only Human Resources Director. And just like that, I was erased. I became a ghost. Gone without a trace.

The Big Shift

Looking back, it's painfully clear. Our company was self-insured. Every surgery, every therapy session, every diagnostic scan, every out-of-network provider I'd fought for came directly out of their pocket. I hadn't just become inconvenient. I had become expensive.

There was one person I thought I could trust; a claims director based in another state, at the Home Office. He was kind. Supportive. He'd given me the green light to pursue the care I needed and never questioned my treatment plan. In fact, he encouraged me to lead it. I believed he saw me. That he was in my corner.

But now, I understand his role differently. He was also the one responsible for reporting high-cost claims. For making sure the numbers were flagged. For alerting the people in power when someone like me was costing too much.

It wasn't cruel. It was clinical. And yet, it left its mark.

At the time, I didn't see it for what it was. There were no alarms. No sharp turns. Just another quiet subtraction I couldn't name. It would take years to surface.

An ordinary day. A passing thought. And suddenly, there it was. A flash of clarity that felt like it had been waiting patiently in the background all along.

Because it had been.

My nervous system had remembered, even when I didn't. Storing the silence. Tracking the absence. Filing away the moment I began to vanish.

Not just from a job. But from the belief that someone was truly in my corner.

To their credit, the company did give me six months of severance. It looked generous on paper. But I recognized the number instantly. It wasn't compensation. It was containment. A padded exit designed to keep me quiet before I remembered I still had a voice.

I met with workers' compensation attorneys. I sat in sterile, beige conference rooms under fluorescent lights, the same cold flicker I remembered from that backroad hospital, listening as phrases like "multi-year litigation," "corporate defense strategy," and "hostile counsel" buzzed around me like static.

And I felt myself slipping into stillness. I had just rebuilt my body. I didn't have it in me to dismantle my soul in court. So I walked away. Not quietly. Not bitterly. But with the kind of peace you earn when you stop asking broken systems to recognize your worth.

Even though I believed in God, I was raised Catholic, and I believed in Jesus, I didn't ask Him for help. Not then. Not yet. I hadn't truly reached for Him, not in the wreckage, not in the rupture, not even in the ache of being erased.

And then came the quiet. Not clarity. Not a plan. Just stillness. A blank, unmarked *terrain* where my old life had collapsed, and nothing new had taken its place.

It would be romantic to say I woke up the next morning with purpose. I had a vision. A path. A calling. But the truth is, I was terrified. Untethered. Floating between who I'd been and who I might become, with no real idea how to survive in that gap.

So I did what I knew how to do: I applied for pharmaceutical sales jobs. The more respectable next step for a high-achieving woman like me. Six-figure salary. Company car. Polished script. However, I was now offering to sell the very system that failed me. This is what my survival had come to.

This wasn't irony. It was self-abandonment dressed as professionalism. It was the quiet betrayal of a woman who had been taught, too many times, that no one was coming. That safety only came from what she could earn, achieve, or endure.

I wore the blazer. Spoke the language. Checked every box. But something in me had shifted. Maybe it was in my nervous system. Maybe it was in my soul.

Whatever it was, they felt it. And so did I.

One by one, the interviews slipped away. That's when it finally clicked: the old world wasn't rejecting me. It was releasing me.

I didn't know what would come next, but apparently, someone else did. One night, I had a dream. But it wasn't just a dream. It was a visitation. Clear. Unmistakable. And it came from the last person I expected.

My grandfather, the most pragmatic man I'd ever known, appeared to me. He had been gone nearly a decade. He was religious but not particularly spiritual. Certainly not someone I imagined would show up from beyond.

But there he was. Not warm. Not nostalgic. But calm. Steady. Certain.

"You'll be a hypnotherapist," he said. "For golfers."

Golfers? I didn't even play golf. Still don't. But maybe that was the point.

My grandfather had loved the game. He and my grandmother lived on the 18th tee of the only golf course on Marco Island, Florida. A man shaped by the Great Depression, he'd started as a butcher, and after retiring early for health reasons, he rebuilt everything. Made it big in Southwest Florida real estate. Created a new life from grit, loss, and reinvention. He knew about second chances. He knew about mental games. And he knew exactly what it took to start again when your first life ends.

In the dream, he didn't waver. He spoke like it was already decided. Like he was simply reminding me of something I had forgotten. He showed me the name. The logo. The entire business model. Everything precise. Branded. Blueprinted.

Mind Links — *Your Link to Excellent Golf.*

I woke up electrified. Not confused. Not curious. *Clear*. It wasn't guidance.

It was an instruction. And deep in my bones; the same bones that had once been shattered-I knew. This was not my imagination. It was my next assignment.

So I got certified. I dove into the world of hypnosis, trauma work, and subconscious rewiring; subjects I had lived *through* long before I ever studied them. And in the Deep South, where anything outside of church and college football raised eyebrows, I opened my doors anyway.

This time, I wasn't trying to fit in. I wasn't asking for permission. I was claiming the power I had nearly lost. And somewhere in that claiming, in the quiet between breath and breakthrough, I remembered Him. Jesus. Not as a figure from childhood, or a doctrine I once learned, but as the companion who had never left. He had been there in the crash, in the silence, in the betrayals, in the dream. I just hadn't known where to look.

But now, something in me had turned toward the light, and I could feel Him again. Not condemning. Not correcting. Just present. Steady. Holding space for the woman I was becoming.

And to my astonishment... it worked.

MindLinks didn't just gain traction. It took off. I was invited to appear on the Golf Channel, featured on the covers of national golf magazines, and asked to teach at the Professional Golfers Career College in Orlando—even though I didn't even play the game.

That became part of my edge.

"I'm not here to teach you how to hit a ball," I would tell clients. "I'm here to help you stop sabotaging yourself when it matters most."

The more I spoke, the more the doors opened. I was invited to speak on the stage at the International PGA Show, the most prestigious event in the golf industry. And then came something that struck a different kind of chord: I was asked to teach at The Annika Academy, founded by Hall of Fame golfer Annika Sorenstam, a woman who had carved her name into a game that rarely made space for women.

Being invited into a sanctuary built by a female icon, for other rising women in the sport, wasn't just an honor. It felt like a quiet kind of redemption. A woman who once shrank to survive was now being trusted to help others expand.

At the PGA Show, I also met Omarosa Stallworth, known from NBC's *The Apprentice*, who later hired me to help resolve a trauma from her youth.

Recognition came fast. But what followed mattered more.

Those moments became one of many that confirmed I was on the right path. What began as golf performance coaching evolved into something far more human.

I wasn't just helping athletes stay calm under pressure. I was helping husbands become better fathers. Wives remembered who they were before burnout. People started to breathe again, not just in their game, but in their lives. And families began to heal...one session, one shift, one person at a time.

A New Path

My work wasn't built in a classroom or modeled after someone else's framework. Long before *functional medicine* had a name, before it was trending, branded, or taught, I was already doing the work.

Back in 2001, in Orlando, a city with Southern values and Northern sprawl, just saying the word *"healing"* out loud was enough to raise suspicion. But I kept going. I pieced together a recovery plan from instinct, desperation, and sheer determination:

- Super Slow resistance training.
- Regression therapy.
- Rebirth practices.
- Breathwork.
- Nutritional protocols I could barely afford.

No prescriptions. No shortcuts. Just food. Movement. Breath. Belief. And, faith.

There were no Instagram wellness experts. No integrative MDs with online dispensaries. Just a few quiet pioneers and my willingness to trust what felt true in my own body, even when no one around me understood. I didn't learn this work from a seminar. I *lived* it. Alone. Without a guide, except a few books pulled off dusty bookstore shelves.

So when I started working with clients, I wasn't handing them a protocol. I was offering a path I had walked barefoot, a system built on survival, devotion, and lived truth. And in the process, I became the person I had once needed so badly:

Someone who could see the *whole* human being, and hold space for a life beyond just surviving.

And then life, it seemed, wasn't done with its ironies. Because after all the gaslighting, the layoff, the trauma, and the so-called "quackery," I fell in love with...and eventually married...a traditional medical doctor. An Emergency Room physician, no less. The very department where my collapse had initially begun. A man trained in science, in systems, in protocols. But also, a man who saw beyond them.

Early in our budding romance, he noticed something in me. Not through lab results. Not through testing. Just presence. "You're low in progesterone," he said one day. "I can tell." He wasn't diagnosing. He was listening, not just with his education, but with his intuition.

He offered to help rebalance my system, not with the usual prescriptions, but with bioidentical hormone replacement therapy. He had already been studying them. Already open to the possibilities outside of allopathic medicine.. Already questioning the boxes medicine had placed around healing. That conversation began a new kind of partnership.

Our work didn't grow because we always agreed. It grew because we stayed at the table, even when it was uncomfortable. He spoke the language of the lab. I spoke the language of the body. And over time, our two distinct vocabularies began to understand each other.

We're still married. And yes, we argue. Not because we're broken, but because I finally have a voice. I don't shrink anymore. I don't disappear to keep the peace. The old fears still visit...fear of being left, fear of being unseen—but I no longer abandon myself to be loved. And in that kind of space that's messy, honest, and alive, our work has never lost its clarity.

I taught him what medicine doesn't always reveal:
• That healing doesn't live in lab results.

- That symptoms are messengers.
- That trauma doesn't always show up on a scan.
- That the body will find a way to speak, especially when no one is listening.

And he taught me something too: That science, when held with humility, can bend toward compassion. It doesn't need to dominate the story. It can choose to join it.

Now, we do the work together. What we offer isn't just clinical support. It's truly personalized medicine tailored to the body that does the speaking. It's the kind of care I wish I'd had when I was collapsing, the care I fought to create when nothing else worked.

Because everything I've lived, everything I've lost, and everything I've reclaimed has become the foundation for what I offer you now.

Not a diagnosis.

Not a protocol.

Not a quick fix.

A mirror.

A guide.

A hand reaching through the silence.

Not to fix you; to remind you that what hurts is not all you are. That healing doesn't mean going back. It means coming home.

So if your spirit is weary, if your body has been

whispering what your heart can't yet name, start here. I'm listening.

And like the One who never stopped waiting for me...I'll be right here when you're ready.

Take the *Reveal the Root* Quiz —and let the truth inside you rise: https://reveal-the-root.scoreapp.com/

Elizabeth Grace Scarcella

Most Gen X women believe exhaustion, brain fog, and overwhelm are just "part of life." They push through silently, unaware that their nervous system, hormones, and emotions are locked in survival mode. That's where I come in.

I help ambitious, high-achieving women reclaim their personal power by uncovering the root cause of their stress, burnout, and self-doubt, whether it stems from nervous system dysregulation, hormonal imbalance, or unresolved emotional patterns.

By blending neuroscience, functional medicine, and faith-rooted healing, I guide women to restore their energy, regulate their stress response, and reconnect with the deep resilience they were created for. The result? They rise into their purpose with clarity, confidence, and strength.

In this book, I share my own journey out of survival and into true healing. Because healing isn't just possible; it's your birthright.

What if your anxiety, fatigue, or brain fog weren't random, but messages pointing you toward what's been unhealed?

The Reveal the Root™ Quiz helps you identify the hidden imbalances driving your stress and exhaustion... whether hormonal, neurological, emotional, or spiritual.

Take the quiz and get a clear starting point for your healing journey. When you know the root, you can finally break free:

https://reveal-the-root.scoreapp.com

Email: support@elizabethscarcella.com

Instagram: @elizabethscarcella

linko.page: @elizabethgrace

Dedication

I dedicate this chapter to my rock, my husband Dan, and my boys Tyler and Caden.

In memory of my Mom.

Thank you all for your love.

— Heather McNally

THREE

LEARNING TO WALK: THE PATH BEYOND THE B.S.

HEATHER MCNALLY

———

Have you ever felt like an animal in the herd? Maybe a goat, a llama, you decide. Just mooooo-ving along, step by step, heading in the same direction as everyone else. You aren't even thinking, you're just there for the ride. The path is well-trodden, the destination unclear, but you follow anyway because that's just what the herd does.

YOU LIKELY DIDN'T CHOOSE to do this. Maybe you don't even realize you're in the herd. No matter what, the idea of stepping away feels impossible. After all, where would you even go?

For many, many years, I heard the word "No." It was the answer to everything I asked.

"Can I go to the store?" No.
"Can I call my friend?" No.
"Can I go to the movies?" No.

I finally stopped asking altogether. What had I learned?

"No, I can't."

The word "No" became my default answer, my automatic response to *everything*.

At 25, I found myself in a conversation with a friend, and when she asked me, "Do you want to...?" But before she even finished sharing where she wanted to invite me as her plus one, I answered using my autoreply, *"No, I can't."*

As the words left my mouth, it was like a brick hit me in the face...Wait! She just asked me to go to a concert that I *want* to attend. Who was that answering with a "No, I can't?"

That wasn't *my* voice. That wasn't *me* talking. I hadn't even processed the question before I spoke. I didn't stop to think, "Do I want to do this?" or "Do I have the option?"

I was living on autopilot. My subconscious was moving me along with the herd, and I was just following on my own sad, boring, disempowered ride.

Breaking Free from Belief Systems

That was an a-ha moment for me. It was as though a dense fog lifted, and I was struck by lightning simultaneously. I saw myself for the first time. Up until that moment, I was living in the "B.S.": the Belief Systems (but yeah, you can think that "other" thing also, LOL) that had been imposed on me for years. These beliefs weren't even mine. They were the ones I'd been taught, the ones I'd absorbed from my parents, teachers, and the world around me.

Did you know that Belief Systems are imposed upon us as children, and that by the age of 7, most of our core beliefs about who we are and the world around us are already in place? At that age, our brains are like sponges, absorbing everything without question. That's because we haven't yet developed the ability to critically analyze or challenge what the adults around us teach us. Our brains just take it all in as fact to help us survive.

And here's the kicker: our brains aren't even fully developed until around the age of 25 (the age I was when I cracked wide open). That means we spend nearly two decades operating under the belief systems we formed as young children, using them to navigate life the best we can. No one sets out to create limiting or disempowering beliefs in us, but as kids, we can't separate truth from perception. Our brains are simply trying to make sense of the world with the information available to us. And that means we often internalize messages that were never meant to define us. Unfortunately, they do, until we wake up and question them.

The Herd Mentality

Growing up, I didn't just live in a household with rules; I was part of a herd. And in this herd, you were required to follow the rules, *without question*. You didn't wander off. You didn't think for yourself. You didn't ask for more. You were expected to stay in line, to accept things as they were, and to never, ever challenge the leader. Questioning the leader was dangerous and led to consequences that I wanted to avoid. And the leader? He was my father.

My home was divided into two. My mother was warm and loving. She did her best to shield me and my brother from my father's anger and cruelty. She fought back in her own way, thinking she was protecting us. But she felt just as trapped as we did.

My father was controlling, critical, and demeaning. He was both physically and emotionally abusive. His voice was the loudest, the most powerful, and the one, I would eventually come to realize, that had shaped my beliefs about myself.

I lived in a contradictory existence.

I learned that I was too much, but also never quite enough. I should dream big, but I should never expect to reach those dreams. I was smart, but not as smart as I should be. I was pretty, but people would use my looks against me to hurt me.

The endlessly conflicting stories were confusing, and they all led to one single truth in my mind: *I wasn't worthy*.

As you might expect, I detested being at home because of my father. I would hide in my bedroom as much as possible to stay out of his sight and, hopefully, out of his mind, too. I spent time losing myself in music, writing poetry, and daydreaming of another life. But deep down, I didn't think I would ever have that life—or that I even truly deserved it. I was depressed. I was angry. Actually, I was quite full of rage. I was hurting. I was disempowered. I felt like I would always be his punching bag physically, verbally, and emotionally. I *couldn't* see a way out. Ever.

One particularly miserable day in my senior year of high school, I cried to my mom in frustration and desperation, "I can't stand this anymore, and I don't know what to do!" She sighed, looked at me, and said, "At least you only have one more year. You're going to college. I have the rest of my life."

That moment *crushed* me. It took my breath away. As much as I hated *my* situation, I realized that she felt powerless, too. She was defeated. She saw no escape. She had accepted that this was her life. And in that moment, I feared that I would, too. Still, I so desperately wanted something different for myself. I ached for it.

Here's the "funny" thing about herd mentality. When you're in it, you don't even realize it. It feels safe. It feels normal. Even when it downright sucks, at least it's familiar. But once you become aware, you start to wake up, you can't unsee the truth.

I started waking up slowly. At first, it was just noticing small things:
- How often I said "I can't" without even thinking
- How often I made myself small
- How often I avoided conflict because I was terrified of it and how it would end.

But I also believed I wasn't worth fighting for. And then, little by little, I started testing my limits. I started saying "yes" when I would have reactively said "no." I started questioning the beliefs I had carried for so long. Were they even mine? Is that what I wanted to say?

Breaking Away from the Pack

To say leaving the herd wasn't easy would be the understatement of the century. It was really, really hard and felt like the world's craziest rollercoaster. It meant feeling and facing fear. It meant unlearning decades of conditioning. It meant standing up for myself in ways I had never even contemplated before. It meant walking away from relationships that kept me stuck. And most of all, it meant choosing myself over and over again until I saw a flicker of the person I always knew I was meant to be.

And then I started to become her.

If any parts of my story resonate with you, I want you to know this: *You are not stuck. You are not powerless. You do not have to stay in the herd.*

The first step is recognizing where you are. Acknowledgment is power. And once you see it, you can begin the journey of stepping out, little by little, until one day, you realize you're no longer following the herd. You're leading yourself.

Now, perhaps this isn't your exact story. Maybe you didn't grow up in a household like mine (I truly hope you didn't). But put yourself in this position: You feel like something is off. You aren't living the way you want to. Maybe you've been aware of it for a long time, or you're just now realizing it. Or you can't quite put your finger on it yet, but deep down, you know *something* is off, you're not fully happy. It could just be a feeling without a name.

We've all been there. We've all felt like we're doing what we're "supposed to" do: following the path laid out for us, even when it doesn't feel right. We follow expectations. We stay in line. We try to please. We avoid rocking the boat. We ignore the inner voice whispering that something is missing.

This is the herd mentality. It's doing what everyone else is doing because it feels safe.

> Because it's what you were taught. Because it's easier than questioning everything and risking being the one to step away.

It feels easier to stay in the herd because everything else seems so scary!

But let me ask you something: Have you ever seen an animal break free from the herd? It's rare, right? Most animals follow blindly, trusting that the herd must know where it's going. But that's the thing. The herd isn't thinking. It's just moving. And if the herd is heading off a cliff, well... they're all going down together.

I know what it feels like to be that herd animal, caught up in the movement, afraid to break away, just going with the motions. And I also know what it feels like to finally step out—to see a new path, to realize I have a choice, to take control of my life in a way I never thought possible.

But as you can imagine, breaking away from the herd isn't easy. Stepping away is scary as hell! It's uncomfortable. It's unfamiliar. And it requires you to start questioning beliefs you've held onto for years, that B.S. that has defined your whole existence.

I started small. I knew I felt something was wrong. I knew I was angry. I knew I was depressed. I had always felt so stuck. I just didn't know that it could change. It took work! I had to rewire my thinking, challenge every automatic "no" that came out of my mouth, and learn how to tune into my own desires. I had to stop seeing myself as just another animal in the herd and start seeing myself as an individual who had the power to make my own choices.

Small Steps Add Up

And that's where you can begin, too—with awareness. Awareness of your beliefs, your patterns, your habits. Awareness of the moments when you say "yes" out of obligation or "no" out of fear. Awareness of when you're following the herd instead of listening to yourself.

It often starts with that feeling that something is just off. That leads to some inkling of what you're actually feeling: unhappy, sad, angry, disempowered, obligated, hurt, etc. Once you become aware, you can't unsee it. It just keeps showing up and poking at you. And that's when everything starts to change.

Now, I invite you to take action. Not just to think about this, not just to nod along, but to take a step forward.

First, take some time to sit down and reflect. Journal about the things in your life that keep coming up in your mind.

• What runs through your thoughts late at night - and often keeps you awake?

• What tugs at your heart and your soul?

• What feels off?

• What is possibly even screaming out to you?

There's actual science behind this, too. When you

physically write something down—pen to paper—it signals to your brain that it's been acknowledged, which can help quiet that endless loop of thoughts running through your mind. It's like your brain says, 'Oh, okay, we're dealing with this,' and it doesn't have to keep bringing it up at two o'clock in the morning. Studies have even shown that handwriting engages different areas of the brain than typing does, helping with processing, emotional regulation, and problem-solving. So when you write, you're not just venting—you're actively giving your brain some relief and clarity.

Now look for the *patterns*. Are you seeing themes in what you're thinking about, and subsequently writing about? Sometimes, we know deep down what isn't working, but often we need to see it in writing before we fully grasp it.

Find Your Superpower

You do NOT have to remain stuck in the herd. You don't have to keep being pushed down a path that isn't yours. You have a choice. *Choosing is your superpower.* Your thoughts lead to your feelings, your actions, and your results. If you don't like the results you're getting in your life, look back at the thoughts you were having. Those thoughts led to your feelings, which you acted upon. You have the power to change those thoughts, thereby changing how you feel, respond, and the results that you get.

Having these realizations and then making new choices and changes isn't *easy*. You may, at times, want to give up. But it is SOOO WORTH IT! Why? Because you become powerful. Because you start living life on *your terms*, fully, embracing what the world has to offer, and offering yourself to the world.

I do not believe in perfection. I don't support toxic positivity. I do, however, believe that every experience teaches you a lesson, and from there you can make empowered, positive decisions for yourself. Feelings are an important part of this life experience. Experience them. But don't "live" in those difficult moments and feelings. Go through them, and then stand up, take the time to look at what lessons you can learn from them. Take those lessons and move forward with purpose. *Make the empowered choice!*

We have this one life to experience. Yours deserves to be a beautiful journey! The saying "Life is a journey, not a destination" by Ralph Waldo Emerson rings true. Often, we get stuck in the "I can't" and "when I get to... " and follow the herd, living out the expectations of others. Is that really how you want to live? Do you want everyone else making your choices for you? Or do you want to live life to the fullest, experiencing your own personal, amazing, fulfilling journey? The choice is yours!

When you are ready to take that first step, I'm here to walk alongside you.

So take a deep breath, shake off the dust, and start listening to that voice inside you.

The one that's been trying to get your attention all along.

The one that knows you're meant to stand out and shine, to step off the path from the herd.

The one that's ready to break free.

And when you do, well, that's when the real adventure begins.

Heather McNally

Heather is a Master Certified Life Coach, keynote speaker, and author with a passion for helping people break through limiting beliefs and create a life filled with happiness, confidence, and fulfillment.

Having overcome childhood abuse, depression, and anxiety, Heather transformed her struggles into fuel for her purpose. She refused to let her past define her and now helps others do the same—turning pain into power and rewriting the stories that hold them back.

Blending psychology, brain science, and real-life experience, Heather helps clients recognize where they're stuck, harness the power of acknowledgment, and rewire their thinking for lasting change.

Her message is simple but profound: true change begins with owning your story and choosing your next chapter. Through her keynote speeches and forthcoming book chapter, she shares her personal journey of self-discovery and transformation, guiding others to step into their full potential.

Beyond her work, Heather is happily married to Dan, her best friend of 29 years, as well as a proud Mom to two college-aged sons, Tyler and Caden. She's an animal lover with a mini zoo of dogs and cats, a passionate fan of music, crafting, theater, everything ocean, travel, and always up for a game night with friends.

With warmth, authenticity, and a deep understanding of human behavior, Heather empowers others to step into the best version of themselves—because the life you deserve is already within reach.

Get your FREE Limiting Belief Finder at https://www.heathermcnally.com

Email: heather@heathermcnally.com

Dedication

For my Husband, you are the love of my life and my safe space.
For my children, Alexa and Ryan, you are my heart and my why.
For my mom and grandma, your belief in me taught me to dream bigger.
To my village, thank you for reminding me I was never alone.
With love,

— Noelle Kustas

FOUR

THE RISE THAT REBUILT EVERYTHING

NOELLE KUSTAS

After 19 years of whispering, "Maybe tomorrow," everything changed in a single, heart-pounding moment.

FOR NEARLY TWO DECADES, I had walked on eggshells, silencing my own needs, making excuses, and hoping that love alone could fix what was broken. But on this night, Mother's Day of all days, a day that should have been filled with love and celebration, everything came to a breaking point. The tension that had been simmering beneath the surface for years erupted. What began as another uncomfortable evening quickly spiraled into a storm of yelling, tears, and chaos, the kind of chaos you can't reason with, the kind you don't fix. It's the kind you survive.

The air grew thick, almost unbreathable, as if the house itself was holding its breath. My heart pounded so violently I could feel it echo in my ears, muffling the noise but not the fear. I had felt this moment approaching in subtle ways, tight shoulders, forced smiles, quiet prayers whispered behind closed doors. But still, I wasn't prepared. Not for *this* night. Not for Mother's Day.

I could feel my son's tiny hand clutching mine, trembling with confusion and fear. His wide eyes mirrored my own, begging for reassurance I couldn't give. Nearby, my daughter appeared from the bathroom, her hair dripping onto her pajamas, her face a mixture of innocence and alarm. She had no idea what was happening, no time to process the whirlwind she had just stepped into.

My instincts took over. I knelt down, locking eyes with her for the briefest moment as if to silently say, *Trust me. We're going to be okay.*

But deep down, I wasn't sure.

This wasn't just a bad night. It was a *breaking* night, the kind that splits your life into a before and after.

We couldn't stay. The walls around us, the life I had clung to for far too long, were no longer safe. Every instinct screamed that if we stayed another second, we might lose something we could never get back, our safety, our spirit, or worse.

Fear gripped me like a vice, tightening with every heartbeat. But then, something deeper surged, a determination I didn't know I had. It was as if a voice long buried whispered in my ear: *"This is your chance. Go now."*

With nothing but my purse, the clothes on our backs, and trembling resolve, I grabbed my children and ran. We stepped into the unknown, leaving behind the only life we'd ever known. We didn't walk out calmly. We ran for our lives.

There was no time to think. I flung open a single car door, and they both scrambled in. My daughter, still dripping from the shower and barefoot in her pajamas, helped her little brother into his car seat with shaking hands. I could hear my own heartbeat pounding louder than my thoughts as I slammed my door shut and threw the car into reverse.

That's when I saw him.

He came running toward the car, screaming, banging on my window, telling me to get out, to get inside. Saying things no one should ever say, let alone in front of children. But I couldn't let him reach us. I couldn't let my children feel that fear for one second longer.

Searching for Safety

I hit the gas and sped out of the driveway, his voice fading behind us but still echoing in my ears.

I had no idea where to go. My mind was spinning. What if he follows us? What if I lead him to someone else? Where is safe? I couldn't risk putting anyone else in danger. So I kept driving, my heart was pounding, and my mind racing.

I turned into a quiet neighborhood and parked in between a row of cars. I shut off the headlights, the dashboard, every light I could. We sat there in the dark, completely still. I wanted the car to disappear. I wanted him to drive past without seeing us. I needed to think. I needed to breathe.

My kids were silently crying in the back seat. Not screaming. Just the quiet, heart-wrenching sound of tears that come when your world shifts too fast to understand. I could barely speak, but I turned to them and whispered the only words I could find.

"We're going to be okay. We're safe now. I promise."

Even if I wasn't sure yet. I needed them to believe it.

Eventually, I turned the engine back on and drove to the one place I knew we'd be safe: my parents' home. I didn't want to burden them. But I knew my kids needed their comfort, and so did I.

That night was traumatic. But it was also the night I knew everything would change. Maybe not immediately. Maybe not easily. But completely. I realized something profound: transformation doesn't happen by chance. It begins with a choice.

A choice to leave.

A choice to believe.

A choice to rise.

The hardest part wasn't stepping away from the life I knew; it was facing the terrifying blank slate that stretched out before me. I had no answers, no guarantees, just faith. Faith that life could be more, that *I* could be more.

Choosing Myself and My Kids

At that moment, I didn't just choose freedom. I chose to rewrite the story I thought was set in stone. It was terrifying. It was exhilarating. And it was the beginning of everything.

I chose freedom. I chose courage. And, in that moment, I chose to become the woman and mother we all deserved.

The first few weeks after leaving were pivotal. When pivots happen, life doesn't just pause, even though you so wish it would. Life goes on, and you have to figure that out in real time. The kids still needed routines. Bills still needed to be paid. Some of the most important lessons I learned came during that blurry transition. It takes a village, and you should never be afraid to lean into that. My brother flew across the country within 48 hours to help. My in-laws were gracious and supportive. My parents were our rocks. With their help, we were able to return to our home once he moved out. My brother rearranged the entire house so it felt like a fresh start. We continued therapy. I went to work. The kids went to school. And I kept making hard decisions. I found strength I never knew I had.

Motherhood has a way of changing you forever. In the quiet moments, when the kids were finally asleep, I would watch them and feel the tears fall. Not from fear anymore, but from all the emotion that still needed a place to land. I was exhausted. But somewhere deep inside, there was an unshakable knowing that we were going to be okay. Single motherhood isn't the easy answer, but it was the only one. It revealed a resilience in me that had been forged through pain and fire. A quiet strength that kept going, even when I wanted to give up.

In the days and months that followed, I realized I wasn't just rebuilding my life, I was rebuilding *myself*. For years, I had been defined by my roles: wife, mother, teacher. But who was I beneath all of that?

The answer didn't come all at once. It came in quiet moments, in the cracks between fear and hope, and in the soft whispers of intuition. I didn't have the words for it then, but three guiding lights began to emerge, pulling me forward: *faith, family, and love.*

Faith wasn't just about spirituality; it was the belief that even though I couldn't see the path ahead, it was there waiting for me. It was trusting that I wasn't alone, that something greater was holding me steady when everything else felt uncertain.

Family wasn't just about being a mom; it was about creating a space where my children and I could feel safe, loved, and able to thrive. It was about redefining what family could look like. It was a partnership of love and unity that included *me* in the equation, not just my children.

And love, oh, love. Love was the most complicated of all. I had poured love into everyone else for so long that I had forgotten how to give it to myself. But even then, in the rawest moments of my journey, I began to see glimmers of what self-love could look like: boundaries, forgiveness, and the courage to let myself dream again.

I didn't call them "core values" at the time. They were simply my compass, my guiding light. These three pillars, faith, family, and love were what I clung to when everything else felt uncertain. They reminded me of who I wanted to become, even when I wasn't sure how to get there.

The idea of freedom came later, as I began to work on myself in a way I never had before. Freedom wasn't just about leaving a marriage or a life that no longer served me; it was about discovering the ability to choose me. It was realizing that I had the power to create a life that aligned with my heart, my dreams, and my values.

Through this process, I discovered something profound: when you start aligning your life with what truly matters, you begin to rebuild not just a life, but a *self*.

Transforming My Future

The road to transformation was anything but smooth. There were moments when fear crept in, whispering to me, *"You're not strong enough. What if you fail?"* But I've learned that resilience isn't built in the easy moments. It's forged in the awkward, messy, *laugh-so-you-don't-cry* moments when you decide to keep going anyway.

One such moment? The online dating adventure.

Nearly two years after I'd sworn off the idea of love, my best friend sat me down and said, "It's time. We're making you a dating profile." I resisted with every excuse I could think of. *Who would even want me? Do you know how long it's been since I've even flirted? What if someone actually messages me?*

But there I was, reluctantly creating a profile that would also have been perfect for selling a used car: *"Slightly worn, but still has potential!"*

When I got my first few matches, panic set in. A message popped up: *"Hi! How's your day?"* And instead of replying like a normal human, I did the only logical thing my brain could muster, I deleted my entire profile. Poof. Gone.

I sat there staring at the empty screen, laughing at myself. I was so out of practice, and it was painfully awkward. But something inside told me, *"Try again. This time, don't take yourself so seriously."*

About a month later, I did. But I eased up on the pressure and gave myself a lot more self-compassion. The next few months were a rollercoaster of growth, clarity, and some truly unforgettable dating experiences. It wasn't perfect, but it was exactly what I needed. And that's when I eventually met him. The one.

From our very first conversation, he made me laugh in a way I hadn't laughed in years. When we finally met in person, I was nervous but determined to be open to trying something new. He suggested oysters, and I didn't have the heart to tell him I'd never tried them before. So there I was, smiling across the table, trying to gracefully choke down a slimy oyster while wondering if this was a test I hadn't studied for. I couldn't decide whether to smile or vomit, but when I looked up, he was grinning at me like I was the most beautiful thing he'd ever seen.

He always says the reason he fell in love with me is because of my smile. And here's the truth: in the past, my smile was a mask, a way to hide the pain I carried. I wore it to survive. But with him, my smile was different. It wasn't forced or painted on. It was real, effortless, and filled with a joy I hadn't felt in years.

That night, I realized something important: *you get to define what bravery looks like.* Sometimes, it's doing the hard, soul-shifting work of healing. And sometimes, it's as simple as saying yes to something uncomfortable and laughing your way through it. Bravery can look like choking down an oyster. It can look like feeling awkward and nervous but showing up anyway.

And yet, that wasn't the last time I would have to be brave.

Another Turning Point

Years later, after I had worked so hard to rebuild my life, I found myself standing at another crossroads. The pandemic had changed so much for so many, and for me, it magnified something I had been quietly trying to ignore: I couldn't keep doing what I was doing.

After 25 years in the classroom, teaching, the career I had once clung to as part of my identity no longer felt aligned. What had once brought me purpose now left me exhausted. Every Sunday afternoon became a ritual of tears, anxiety, and dread as I prepared for another week I no longer had the heart for.

One day, my husband, who by this point had been by my side for several years looked at me, his eyes filled with love and concern, and said something that stopped me in my tracks. *"If you don't do something different, we're going to be sitting here every Sunday, in the same place, with the same tears."*

It wasn't harsh. It was honest. And at that moment, I remembered that *I still matter*. That it is okay to choose something different, even in my late 40s. Life doesn't have to end and I can have my encore.

This time, the fear was different. I wasn't running away from something. Instead, I was giving myself permission to evolve and step into a new version of myself, even though it terrified me.

Walking away from teaching was one of the hardest decisions I've ever made. It had been my identity for so long. It was what held me up during some of my darkest moments. But deep down, I knew I was being called to something greater. I wanted to create something that would allow me to use my voice, my story, and my heart to empower other women walking through their own transitions. I decided to start a business that would help women rediscover their purpose, rebuild their confidence, and step into a life they love.

Starting my own business felt like jumping into the unknown all over again. It was terrifying, exhilarating, and completely outside my comfort zone.

With every step, I proved to myself that I was capable of so much more than I had ever believed. And as I look back on that journey, I can't help but smile. Not just because I took those brave steps, but because this smile, this life, and this encore chapter are truly *mine*.

This wasn't just about transforming my life, I was stepping into my purpose. Each new, brave step I took, each moment I chose to believe in myself, was a step toward becoming the woman I was always meant to be.

Helping women rediscover their confidence, reconnect with their identity, and step into lives that light them up has become my *why*. I've lived the fear, the doubt, and the pain of thinking, *"Maybe this is all there is."* But I've also felt the power of deciding that *no, there's more*.

Today, this business I built, this mission I live in feels like home. It's confirmation that I am exactly where I'm supposed to be. Every time I sit across from a woman and witness her reclaim her worth, her voice, her spark, I know without a doubt this is what I was meant to do.

I see women differently now. I see what's underneath their titles and to-do lists. I see the quiet strength in their eyes, the stories behind their smiles, the courage it takes just to keep showing up. I see them through a lens shaped by everything I've walked through, and I don't take that gift lightly.

These days, sipping my morning coffee has become more than a routine. It's a ritual. A quiet moment of gratitude for the life I once dreamed of and the one I now get to live. Gratitude for the journey, not just the destination. Gratitude for what was, what is, and what is still becoming.

This life is more than I could have ever hoped for.

Your Future: Reimagined

And I share that not to say it was easy, but to show you what's possible. Healing is possible. Joy is possible. A life that feels safe, sacred, and fully yours is possible.

This isn't just my story, it's yours.

What dream have you been putting on hold? What whisper keeps telling you, *"There's more for you"*? Maybe you're standing at a crossroads, unsure of which way to go. Or maybe you're quietly wondering if it's too late to start over. I want you to know this: *It's never too late to choose you.*

You are worthy. You are enough. And you have a purpose.

It's not reserved for the lucky few. It's within you, waiting to be uncovered. It's in the quiet moments when you let yourself dream. It's in the brave decisions, the messy steps forward, and the belief that your best chapter is still ahead.

What would it look like to step into your purpose today? Not tomorrow. Not next week. *Today.* Maybe it's taking one small step toward a goal. Maybe it's choosing to believe in yourself, even when it feels hard. Whatever it is, I want you to know this: transformation is possible for you, just as it was for me.

On the night I chose freedom over fear. I walked out into the unknown with nothing but my purse, my children, and the hope that life could be better. It wasn't easy. It wasn't without pain. But it was the beginning of something extraordinary.

In choosing myself, I didn't just change my life, I changed *ours*. Today, my children and I are thriving. Our family is a reflection of the choices I made to prioritize faith, love, and freedom. My daughter has grown into a resilient, compassionate woman, and my son who once clung to my hand so tightly has grown into a confident young man.

Freedom has become the compass for my next chapter. At first, it meant survival, leaving behind what was no longer safe. But over time, it became something deeper. Now, freedom means living with intention, choosing what aligns with my heart, and building a life anchored in faith, love, and the family we've fought so hard to rebuild.

You have one life, and it's never too late to rewrite your story.

Maybe it's taking one small, brave step toward a goal that's been quietly waiting in your heart. Maybe it's choosing to believe in yourself, even when fear whispers otherwise. Maybe it's simply giving yourself permission to dream again. Transformation begins with a single choice. It won't always be easy, but I promise you this: it will be worth it. The chapter ahead of you holds more than you can imagine. Life isn't over. It's your encore.

Before you turn the page, take a quiet moment with yourself.

Close your eyes and ask: *What choice are you willing to make today to step into the life you deserve? What does freedom feel like to me now?* What does faith look like in this season? What kind of love do I want to give and receive? What kind of life am I ready to claim?

You don't need all the answers today.

But you do deserve to ask the questions.

Because the life that lights you up?

It is already waiting for you to say yes.

When you choose yourself, you shift everything.

When you choose freedom, you make room for joy, for healing, for something beautifully new.

And that is where the magic begins.

You are not alone.

You are seen.

And I cannot wait to witness what you create next.

With all my heart,

Here's to your next chapter...

–Noelle, Your Spark Igniter

Noelle Kustas

Noelle Kustas is a mentor, speaker, podcaster, and founder of Rise2Shine Co. and The Glow Up Mentoring School for Midlife Mamas. With over 25 years as an educator, she now empowers midlife women to rediscover their purpose, embrace their next chapter with confidence, and create a life they love. Through her signature programs, podcast, speaking engagements, and transformative mentorship, Noelle helps women rise above limiting beliefs, reclaim their spark, and step into their next season with joy.

Her own journey of resilience and reinvention fuels her passion for helping others, and she is known as The Spark Igniter for her ability to inspire breakthroughs. Noelle's work has impacted countless women, reminding them that midlife is not an ending, it's the beginning of their most powerful chapter yet.

Based in Southern California, Noelle loves spending time with family and friends, sharing heartfelt conversations over coffee, and traveling, especially to places where the water sparkles and the air is filled with possibility.

Get The Glow Up Blueprint: A Guide to Clarity, Confidence, and Purpose for Midlife Women (35+)

Midlife isn't a time to fade into the background, it's your encore, and it's time to make it extraordinary. The Glow Up Blueprint is designed for women 35+ who are ready to gain clarity, rediscover what lights them up, and step into this next chapter with confidence and purpose.

Inside, you'll learn how to:

Break free from overwhelm and create a simple, actionable plan for what's next.

Reignite your passion and uncover what truly makes you feel alive.

Use powerful tools to take meaningful action—without overthinking or second-guessing yourself.

This isn't just another guide, it's your invitation to step into the woman you've always known you were meant to be. Your time is now.

Download The Glow Up Blueprint today and start designing a life that feels truly like yours: https://rise2shine.co/glowupblueprint

Podcast: https://www.youtube.com/@Rise2ShinePodcast
Email: noelle@rise2shine.co
Website: rise2shine.co
Instagram: https://www.instagram.com/joyful_noelle
Facebook: https://www.facebook.com/NoelleKustas/
Linkedin: www.linkedin.com/in/noellekustas

FIVE

BEAUTIFULLY BROKEN (BROKEN BUT NOT FULLY HEALED)

HEATHER OLSON

On a sunny morning in March, I made a plan to end my life.

THE THOUGHT of having to keep going was just too unbearable. But since I had already committed to a playdate for my children, my plan would have to wait until the afternoon. Not showing up to the playdate would have made me (this young, people-pleasing woman) sick to my stomach. Also, I wanted to give my then 2-year-old and 8-month-old boys one last happy memory of me.

That morning, my children and I met another mom and her kids at a local gymnastics facility. She and I sat with our babies, making small talk, while our older children ran around. Suddenly, out of the corner of my eye, I noticed my 2-year-old struggling in the giant foam pit. He was sinking and couldn't keep his head above the foam.

That single moment changed my life, but not the way you might expect.

In an instant, I scooped up my little one and lurched toward my older son. But in my haste to get to him, I stepped down onto what I thought was solid ground but turned out to be the springs of the in-ground trampoline. Almost immediately, my leg buckled, I felt a snap, and I crumpled to the floor.

My friend looked down at me lying there and asked, "Are you ok?" I said, "No, I think I just broke my leg". My friend jumped up and ran to get help.

Before the Break

In the months leading up to that fateful moment, I had been struggling with postpartum depression. The ups and downs throughout the day when breastfeeding were becoming almost unbearable, and before long, I was so depressed that I started having suicidal ideations.

I had not experienced these scary thoughts with my first son. But after doing research and reading about my symptoms, I now know that my experience is not uncommon. These symptoms become more likely with each additional child.

My second baby was born in July, and by the middle of the following January, my husband encouraged me to get some help. The doctor prescribed me antidepressants, and I started taking them right away.

Within a few weeks, I was feeling much better. A month into taking the medication, I started feeling like myself again. Naturally, I thought I was better. So, without consulting my doctor, I made the executive decision to stop taking the medication entirely. This would prove to be one of the biggest mistakes of my life.

A Dark Turn

Almost instantly, I spiraled into an even deeper and darker depression than I had experienced before. The suicidal ideation came back and was stronger than ever. The night before that fortuitous playdate, my husband and I argued about something insignificant, and our conversation was weighing heavily on my mind. As I ruminated about the fight, I became convinced that my husband and boys would be better off without me.

As I lay on the dirty blue trampoline floor, waiting for help to arrive, even my throbbing leg could not stop my mind from racing. How are we going to pay for this? I worried. We did not have insurance. I began to feel ill thinking about the cost and tried to convince myself that I was fine. No broken leg here. But when I tried to get up, it was clear that I would need to go to the hospital.

The Hospital Experience

If you think taking a family of four to Disneyland is costly, try taking an ambulance ride. I was loaded into the vehicle on a gurney and then took the most expensive 3-minute ride of my life to the hospital. When you are in that much pain, each minute takes forever, and I felt every single bump in the road. The morphine *finally* kicked in just before the ride ended.

I was wheeled into the emergency room, where a male nurse told me he was going to need to cut my pants off so the doctors could x-ray my leg. My cheeks turned bright red, and I felt a wave of panic rush over me. At that time, I was in my commando era and had no underwear on. A woman staff member soon walked in to check my pain medication, and I took the opportunity to lean over to her and whisper, "he said that they need to cut off my pants, but I am not wearing any underwear." She chuckled a little and said, "It is okay, honey, we have seen it all."

The medical staff explained, after looking at the first X-ray of my leg, that it was not broken. Instead, they said, my leg was just out of place and needed to be reset. Two painful resets later, a third X-ray determined that my leg was, in fact, broken in four places. The orthopedic surgeon from the nearby hospital came to look over my scans and told me I would need a surgery in which he would put a plate and fourteen screws into my leg to repair it. When the surgery was over, the doctor informed me I would need to be on bed rest for the first month and keep weight off my leg for an additional two months.

As you can imagine, being on bed rest made it impossible for me to care for my two young boys. My step-sister moved in to help take care of the boys and me while my husband was at work during the day. It was while she was there caring for me that I had an epiphany: all this time, I had been neglecting myself, and as it turned out, self-care was exactly what I needed.

Divine Intervention

For reasons I am not even fully aware of yet, I believe that through divine intervention, God saved my life that day for a greater purpose. Once my leg healed, I started prioritizing my health and caring for myself. Just four months after breaking my leg, my husband and I decided to go on a twelve-mile round-trip hike in the Sawtooth Mountains for our anniversary. It was very challenging with my ankle in a brace. We stopped along the way a few times so I could soak my swollen foot and ankle in the cold mountain creek (it was purely snow melt).

That trip was a defining moment in my healing journey. It was the first time I had left my boys overnight. One minute, I was crying because I missed them, and in the next, I was thankful that I was able to get away and recharge my batteries. During that time away, I realized how important it was for me, as a stay-at-home mom, to get out of the house and have time apart from my boys. Then, I could come back home and be a better mom to them.

In the fourteen years since the day I broke my leg, I have adopted a holistic healing approach. I understand the importance of healing the whole self, mind, body, and spirit.

With my spirituality being at the forefront of that healing journey, my higher power being God (you fill in what that is for you). God has taken me on a journey over those years to learn what I need to grow and heal the areas of myself that need healing, while knowing exactly the timing for it. God's timing is not our timing, but He is always right on time.

My Healing Journey

One of the first areas of my life that I changed was with exercise. I can distinctly correlate the times that I have struggled most with my mental health with seasons in my life that I was not prioritizing working out. I don't mean high-intensity, super-strenuous exercise, either. It could be a twenty-minute walk outside. I have found that moving my body at least three days a week helps keep my mental health in good condition. In the immortal words of Elle Woods, "Exercise gives you endorphins. Endorphins make you happy. Happy people don't shoot their husbands, they just don't."

God also showed me that another area I needed to change was with clutter. Words cannot express how freeing it was to declutter my house. As I started clearing junk, the freer I felt in my mind, body, and spirit. It is amazing how much the extra stuff lying around our house weighs us down. In the words of Marie Kondo in her book *The Life-Changing Magic of Tidying Up: The Japanese Art of Decluttering and Organizing*, an item should "spark joy" when you hold it. If it doesn't, get rid of it. Here is your permission to get rid of the things that are no longer serving you or bringing joy to your life.

Eating healthy is another area where I was lacking, and I'm still working on it. I have personally felt the effect that choosing unhealthy foods has had on my mental health. One night a few years ago, we ate fried chicken for dinner. Shortly after that meal, my anxiety went through the roof. At the time, I did not think much of it, but a couple of months later, the same thing happened, and I don't believe in coincidences. I knew that there had to be a correlation between my anxiety and the fried chicken. I immediately started avoiding fried foods.

Since then, I have noticed a difference in my anxiety. Recently, I was speaking with a friend, anxiety expert, and a co-author of *RISE*, Elizabeth Scarcella. She told me that all seed oils can cause anxiety because of the endocrine disruptors in them. These oils can make your hormones unbalanced, which can affect your mood, causing anxiety and depression.

Suddenly, it all made sense to me. I have been living in this loop for years. Eating poor-quality foods has kept me stuck in my anxiety and depression, unable to break free.

We are only now beginning to understand the link between our gut health and brain health. The more I read and hear about it, the more it makes sense why I suffered with debilitating anxiety and depression for so long.

Sleep is another important part of my healing journey. When my kids were younger, I noticed that I was in a worse mental state on the days when I did not sleep well the night before. And as anyone who has had small children knows, that ends up being most of the time. I dove in deep and started reading countless studies on how to optimize my sleep to get the best possible rest. As a result, we now keep our house at a temperature of 64 degrees at night, we have blackout shades on our windows, and we run a fan for white noise and to keep the air circulating.

The most difficult part of my healing journey has been confronting all of the past hurts in my life, forgiving those people, and forgiving myself. The hardest one of these was when God had me look in the mirror and offer myself forgiveness for wanting to end my own life. The tears started rolling down my face before the words even left my mouth.

I fully understand that your healing journey will be different from mine. None of the claims that I have made have been proven to treat or cure depression or anxiety. I'm simply sharing some of the things that have helped me on my journey in hopes that it might help light the path for you or someone you know who is struggling to begin a healing journey, whether it's with therapy, medication, or alternative therapies.

However healing looks for you, I'm here for you and I will be your biggest cheerleader along the way. If you need someone to listen to you, I am always here to listen without judgment.

If you or someone you know is suffering from suicidal ideation or thoughts of self-harm, please reach out for help:

Dial 9-8-8 for the Suicide & Crisis Lifeline or go online at 988lifeline.org.

ABOUT THE AUTHOR: HEATHER OLSON

Heather Olson

Heather is a speaker, author, friend, and she has a heart to serve others. She possesses firsthand experience with postpartum depression and other mental health struggles. She is passionate about helping others find their path to healing.

She believes that there is healing power in sharing your story. Not only for yourself but for others. She encourages everyone to find someone they trust to share their story with. The first time is the hardest but also the most healing.

The titles that she cherishes the most are wife to her husband Brian and mother to her sons Easton, Elijah, and Stanley. She is always ready to embark on their next adventure together.

Learn more: https://heatherrenae.kit.com/

SIX

FIND YOUR VOICE, SHARE YOUR STORY

MELANIE HERSCHORN

Lots of people in the publishing industry will tell you that they were voracious readers as children, holed up in a makeshift reading nook with their nose in a book at all times. That was definitely not me. While many can't remember life before literacy, I do, vividly.

WHEN I WAS in 2nd grade and still struggling, I recall trying to read a chapter book to myself one night before bed. Every other sentence, I would have to yell out across the house, "Mom, what does (fill in the blank) spell? Needless to say, I still don't really know what *Jacob Two Two and the Hooded Fang* is about.

Once I became more adept at spelling out the words, I still had to contend with my extremely slow reading abilities. So I shied away from books and found my escape with Barbie dolls and TV sitcoms.

But in 4th grade, something happened. I reluctantly picked up *Just As Long As We're Together* by Judy Blume at a Scholastic Book Fair. I dreaded those book fairs because they were yet another reminder of how bad I was at reading. But I bought the book anyway. When I got home, I pulled it out of my backpack and put it on my bedside table. That night before bed, I started reading. To my amazement, I did not crave to be able to watch the story unfold on a screen. Instead, I had such beautiful visuals dancing around in my mind's eye. Each character seemed so real to me, and the story resonated so deeply.

Just As Long As We're Together sat on my nightstand for the next 3 years. Every day or so, I would pick it up, turn to a random page, and start reading. It was the book that not only made me fall in love with reading, but with storytelling as a whole.

My Mission Possible

It took me many years to determine my mission. Words have always been my jam. I love adverbs (weird, right?). I have been accused of using multisyllabic words too frequently and sounding like a word snob. I even own socks that shout I'm silently correcting your grammar. The truth is, I am.

Words (on the page and the ones you use in your

videos) can lead to great business success. They can also cause some not-so-great challenges.

> Your words have amazing power so choosing the right words to use to describe your business, your offers, programs, and courses, your book, and everything else you do is wildly important.

No matter what direction my career has veered toward, messaging has been front and center for me. My route to get where I am today was rather nonlinear. When I graduated from college, I ran away from Canada to Los Angeles to work in Hollywood. I spent a few years writing press releases, walking A-list and B-list celebrities down red carpets, attending movie premieres, and hanging out backstage at notable talk shows. But I yearned for more and headed back to school at age 26 to get a master's degree in broadcast journalism.

My first job out of graduate school was working as an afternoon news anchor and general assignment reporter at a radio news station in central Pennsylvania. I was the only woman in a newsroom of men and felt like a fish out of water coming from LA to a small city of just 50,000 people. At radio station-sponsored events, which I was obligated to attend, I would often get backhanded compliments from guests (read: big donors) like, "You're sounding a bit better," or "You don't sound as new anymore," and sometimes outright insults about me and my reporting. At least no one ever told me I had a face for radio!

Whenever I misspoke live on the air, my news director would come running toward me from the newsroom, ready to reprimand me. Since the entire radio booth was glass, I knew ahead of time when I was about to "get it." With such constant scrutiny (one senator's campaign manager spent 20 minutes screaming at me over a misunderstanding), I developed a pretty thick skin. I soon stopped worrying about what other people thought of me because I realized that no matter what I did, I could not please everyone.

Storytelling For The Voiceless

Armed with that protective shell, I decided to pursue a new purpose: to tell the stories of those whose voices deserved to be heard. While I still covered the stories assigned to me, whenever my news director gave me an inch of freedom, I would highlight issues about women, children, veterans, and older people, doing my best to give them a voice on our airwaves.

Some of the in-depth reports included stories such as a story on a camp for young children who had lost a parent or sibling, a series on the wives of senatorial candidates, and a three-part story on teens stuck in and aging out of the Pennsylvania foster care system. I'm proud to say that these stories garnered journalism awards, but the most rewarding part was the gratitude from those featured in the stories. As "talent," I was often asked (read: told) to attend station events. The first time I was required to give a speech, I couldn't bear the thought of talking about myself. I was a journalist - we are never supposed to be part of the story.

So I compiled the stories of the inspirational people whom I had featured in my news reports and shared those:

• The Korean war veteran, who'd lost part of his jaw in combat, shared his vivid and chilling memories.

• The Priest who, at 99, was still giving sermons and delighting his congregants with stories of the scripture and the past.

• The civil rights activist whose father was the Alabama attorney who represented Rosa Parks.

These stories stay with me to this day.

After working at the station for about two years, my husband and I began thinking about growing our family. I knew that having a baby would be frowned upon, so we waited to start trying until a non-election year. I reasoned that at least my three-month maternity leave would not interfere with election reporting. When I was five months pregnant with my first child, I was abruptly laid off from the station. At that point in my life, my entire identity had been wrapped up in being a journalist, and without that position, I felt like I was nothing. What's more, reporters from other news outlets began calling me to ask why I had been laid off so they could include it in their outlets. I had become the story.

As luck would have it, I was not unemployed for long. The local newspaper scooped me up and brought me on to cover an inner-city school district with serious budgetary woes. So, I was still able to report and give a voice to the voiceless. When my daughter was about eight months old, we moved to Arizona. This was a turning point in my career. I knew that any job in journalism would pay me less than I would be paying for childcare, so I opted to answer the call of entrepreneurship, which had been tapping on my heart loudly.

Udderly Hot Mama

Within a year, I launched a line of breastfeeding shirts and dresses for nursing moms. Not really a normal trajectory, I know. I was a breastfeeding mom, and I wanted to help other women in my shoes feel good about themselves during the so-called fourth trimester by offering clothing that was both fashionable and functional. So you could say I was giving clothes to the clothes-less. I single-handedly grew the brand, and within a few years, my products were being sold in boutiques across North America, on Amazon, and Nordstrom's website. My favorite part of the business was marketing, and I wanted to improve my skills. So, in the 7th year of business, I hired a so-called "marketing expert."

This woman I knew claimed to be an internet

marketing expert who could help me make my brand a household name. Unfortunately, that was the beginning of the end of my company. She became verbally and emotionally abusive toward me, constantly telling me that my ideas were boring and that there was no way I could ever do the marketing myself. "How is it that you have a master's degree in journalism?" she would ask. You might be thinking, But Melanie, *you hired her!* You could have severed ties at any time. This woman had me believing that not only did I need her, but that there would also be repercussions if I tried to sever our working relationship. In less than a year, I paid her upward of $25,000.

When it was finally over, I had:

• grown my Instagram following by about 5,000 followers with people who never had and were never going to buy what I was selling

• the belief that everything I wrote was boring and that I was not smart enough to do marketing for my business without her

• experiences of verbal and emotional abuse that made me too fearful to stand up for myself in case she tried to do a smear campaign against my company

It became too difficult for me to keep the business going. My heart was no longer in it. I couldn't even open the door to my home office without getting a sinking feeling in my stomach. Within the year, I had closed up shop.

Mission Found

It took me a beat to figure out what my next move would be. I had some decisions to make. Should I go back to the 9-to-5 or continue the entrepreneurial journey? After some serious introspection and talking with friends, I resolved to turn that awful experience into something positive. I found my voice and my mission again.

When I looked back at my career up to that point, I saw that I had truly developed a skill set to support business owners with their marketing. I also tallied that I had logged about 10,000 hours of marketing, a figure that author Malcolm Gladwell has made famous in his book *Outliers: The Story of Success* as the number of hours it takes to achieve world-class expertise at a particular skill.

My goal was to ensure that other business owners would no longer be misled by marketers making all sorts of promises. Over time, the mission has evolved to focus on helping authors amplify their voices. And I do this with honesty and integrity, always.

Once I hung out the proverbial shingle that I was open for business, authors started calling and asking if I could help market their books. And my foray into the publishing world began. I started out as a book marketer, assisting authors who didn't know the first thing about creating buzz for their books. I worked with a variety of wonderful writers in genres including business books, self-help, spiritual guidance, and children's books. I even partnered with a prolific fiction author whose fantastical novels were developing a big following.

As I became more enveloped in the book world, I knew it was time for me to finally publish my own book. But this was a tall order. I had been wanting to write a book since I fell in love with that Judy Blume novel in the 1980s. But I never followed through.

In graduate school, my professor recommended I turn my thesis into a book, but I'm relieved I didn't take his advice. The subject matter was "niche online dating," and dating apps had not yet been invented. That book would have been obsolete the second it was published! There was also something else stopping me all those years: I questioned my authority. "Who am I to write a book on (fill in the blank)?" And that inner critic kept me small.

The thing was, I was marketing myself as someone who could help authors. But I was not an author. That felt disingenuous to me. So I started writing. Very slowly. I had already developed a program that I took clients through, which was garnering great results, so I used that as my outline. Still, it took me almost 3 years to write and publish my first book.

Part of what stalled me was finding a publisher to

bring my baby to the masses. I knew that I did not want to spend years pitching to a traditional publisher because I was aiming for this book to be a marketing tool, not a New York Times bestseller. So I opted to work with a hybrid publisher. You pay them, they publish under their imprint, and split the royalties with you. It seemed fair. But throughout the process, I started to get a bad feeling.

One night, while I was reading on my Kindle in bed, my eyes had reached the bottom of a page, but I had not read a single word. Something was weighing on me, but I didn't know what. I thought for a moment and realized it was about my book. I couldn't quite put my finger on it, but the woman who ran this hybrid publishing house was saying and doing things that felt like empty promises.

At that moment, I sat up and said out loud, "I don't trust her with my book!"

The next morning, I canceled our contract. I did not even ask for the money back because I knew it was more important to have my intellectual property than to fight her to return the funds.

So there I was, my manuscript back in my hands, but unsure of what to do next. And that is when I resolved to become a publisher too, so that I could continue to combat the predatory behavior that happens in the publishing world, one book at a time. The way we do publishing at Big Impact Books is always transparent and supportive.

We are an independent publisher so we help our clients publish under their own imprint, enabling them to retain all their rights and royalties. We want the process to be as simple and streamlined as possible.

Overcoming The Odds

The scariest part of writing a book, in my opinion, is the moment that you decide you are going to do it. It's the moment that you make a contract with yourself to do something that has been tapping on your heart for a long time but you've been trying to quiet it down with thoughts like:

- Who would read my book anyway?
- Do I really have anything important to say?
- What if it's bad and I'm embarrassed?
- What if my friends and family don't support me?
- What could I write about that hasn't been written before?

And the list goes on. I've had many of these thoughts, too. So have my bestselling author clients. But what separates them (and hopefully you) from the high percentage of people who start writing but never publish is the belief that their mission can help the world, even if it's just one person at a time.

For centuries, people have sat around fires, telling stories to explain natural phenomena. Stories are how we, as humans, learn and remember. Your story is special, and it helps differentiate you from everyone else. I believe wholeheartedly that it deserves to be shared.

To help you get started, here is a free resource to begin planning your bestselling book. Get the Ultimate Book Planning Checklist here: yourbigimpactbook. info/ultimate-book-planning-checklist.

And if you want to discover your book's big idea with help from AI, click here: yourbigimpactbook. info/gpt.

ABOUT THE AUTHOR: MELANIE HERSCHORN

Melanie Herschorn

Known for helping attorneys and business owners become bestselling authors and get positioned as experts in their practice area, Melanie Herschorn wants to help you step into your spotlight as an authority. As a publisher and book marketing strategist, she's on a mission to empower new authors to make an impact and grow their income with their signature books.

With her comprehensive background as a celebrity publicist, an award-winning journalist in radio, print, and TV, and a clothing designer and entrepreneur, Melanie is uniquely positioned to support authors in developing their online presence, building a vibrant audience, stepping into thought leadership, and making a big impact with their book. She earned a Master of Arts in Journalism from the Annenberg School for Communication and Journalism at the University of Southern California, where she graduated first in her class.

Melanie grew up in Canada and has lived on both U.S. coasts. She currently lives in Arizona with her husband, daughter, and son; her Cavalier King Charles Spaniel, Marty McDog; and her Siberian cat, Phoebe.

SEVEN

FROM CLINGING TO CALLING: THE SACRED ART OF LETTING GO AND LIVING BRAVE

CHARITY MAJORS

There is a peculiar ache that lives in the space between what was and what could be. It's the ache of the in-between. The holy, haunting tension of transition.

MAYBE YOU KNOW IT: that restless longing when the old season doesn't fit anymore, but the new one hasn't fully arrived. It's a liminal ache, a divine discontentment, a stretching of the soul, an invitation to trust God when the map is blank and the road ahead is foggy.

I remember learning about letting go before I had words for transition or calling. I was a little girl on the monkey bars, hands slick with sweat and playground dust, arms trembling as I dangled high above the wood chips. The sun beat down on my back, and the laughter of other children faded into a blur as I realized my strength was running out. "Daddy!" I called, my voice thin and desperate, swallowed by the summer air. "Help me! I can't hold on!"

I couldn't see him. My eyes were fixed on the next bar, on the ache in my hands, on the dizzying drop below. But I heard him. His voice, strong and gentle, cut through the chaos: "Charity, you can let go. I'm right behind you. I won't let you fall."

Tears blurred my vision. "But Daddy, I can't see you! How do I know you'll catch me?"

His answer was steady, unwavering: "You can hear my voice. You can trust me. I'm right here. I won't let you fall."

My knuckles turned white as I clung tighter, every muscle burning with the effort to stay suspended. The world shrank to the width of that bar, the ache in my hands, the sound of his voice. Fear screamed, "What if you fall? What if he's not really there?" My strength was gone. With nothing left but trust, I let go. For a split second, I was weightless—caught between fear and faith, earth and sky. And then, just as he promised, my father's arms caught me. I landed not on the hard ground, but in love that would never let me fall.

My dad looked at me with deep smile lines, and I could feel the delight in his heart.

He then said, "Love bug, I'm so proud of you... Today, you learned about trust."

Now, all grown up as a wife, mom, founder, author, speaker, and recovering plant killer, the stakes I now "play with" are much bigger than monkey bars.

The monkey bars turned into boardrooms and business plans. I built a business and brand that sparkled on the outside - the clients, influence, and a calendar bursting at the seams. Rung by rung, people saw a woman who had "arrived."

But inside, I was shrinking. I learned to read the room, to say what was expected, to keep the most vibrant parts of my faith and what I believed tucked away. My brand wasn't faith-based, and my heart longed to live out the call God has on my life as a prophetic voice and revivalist.

But in the business world, my message had to be "safe." I became a master at blending in—never too much, never too bold, always just enough to maintain expert status but not enough to truly stand in my calling.

Now, you may be thinking, "so what...plenty of businesses aren't faith-based..." Or maybe "just keep your personal beliefs and your business separate...or "you can still build your business and be a Christian" without talking about God a lot..."

And I get that... I told myself that for a long time, while I still built but little by little, this stacked more and more bricks around my voice and heart.

And so, *brick by brick*, I tucked my faith and the call on my life away.

Brick by brick, I stifled my voice and what I wanted to boldly share.

Brick by brick, I shrank into a box that suffocated the fire God had placed in my bones.

I called it wisdom, but when I stopped lying to myself, I saw it actually was fear. Fear of being misunderstood. Fear of being "that person." Fear of losing credibility in a world that values polish over presence. Events that scream build your own empire instead of Kingdom Come. Influencers who all say "look at me" when I want my life to point to Jesus.

No one saw the nights I lay awake, haunted by the moments I'd swallowed my words, the times I'd felt the Holy Spirit stirring but stayed silent. Each time I chose safety over surrender, my soul shrank a little more.

But behind the bricks, divine discontentment began to bubble up.

I wrote about this "divine discontentment" in my bestselling book, *Meant For More*, and I explained it as "the moment you realize that you are evolving beyond what you are currently doing, and you are being drawn to the 'what's next' in your life. It's the time when what used to excite you no longer brings you into a state of joy. It's when you start to dread waking up in the morning to go and do what you've been doing. It's the feeling that there is *more* in store..." (page 111 of

Meant For More: Igniting Your Purpose in a World that Tries to Dim Your Light).

> Even though I have felt the divine discontentment before, it seemed as though it was stirring again despite my best efforts to settle into a space and industry for the long haul.

I spent months wrestling with the divine discontentment.

Nights spent with the silence of my soul that spoke volumes.

The stirring of the fire of the Spirit I refused to voice.

Each time I chose safety over surrender to my calling, my soul shrank a little more.

And I *knew* it.

As the ache of the divine discontentment grew and grew, and I (again) started to ask the *big* questions...

The "*Is this what I'm made for?*"

"*Am I truly fulfilled?*"

"*What's the call that God has on my life?*"

"*Where have I been betraying myself and the truth of what I know?*"

"*Do I really want to be known and remembered for this?*"

I started to wonder if the very thing I was hiding was the thing God wanted to use.

It's a strange thing, isn't it? To climb the ladder and feel yourself shrinking. To win by the world's rules and realize you're losing yourself. To be celebrated for what you do, while the truest parts of who you are remain unseen and unheard. The world applauded my hustle and my highlight reel, but the fire God placed in my bones was suffocating. I was living in a box. One I had built, one that looked like success, but one that was slowly suffocating my soul.

I could no longer deny the divine discontentment... I could no longer stay in the box that I had built...

I *had* to break free...

But breaking free meant burning it down.

It meant letting go of everything I was, what I poured my blood, sweat, and tears into, that I built for the unknown of "The Call" on my life.

I could no longer stay where I had been...and so I began to let go...

But before I could let go, I had to remember who I was called to be and where I was called to go. I had to go back into the part of my heart I had closed off while I built my business.

You see, in the midst of building my company, this Calling began to take the back burner.

I had lost the capacity to do the ministry I was called to do, and started to focus solely on business, which had been a really taxing and draining thing lately. Things were definitely out of alignment.

During that time, I slowly tucked those ministry dreams and what God created me for into the back closets of my heart and boarded them up behind delay, disappointment, and discouragement. I buried them behind the "safe" business front and brand voice.

I told myself, "Maybe, one day..." but my maybes started to turn into "probably nots..." and distant disappointments as my business (and the box around me) grew.

I remember one night in church so vividly–the air heavy with the tangible presence of the Holy Spirit, worship music rising and falling around me like a warm current. I sat in my seat, heart pounding, and felt the ache inside me: God tugging at what I knew had to change. I sensed it was time to shift from business into ministry, but fear pressed heavily on my chest.

I was afraid of being misunderstood. I worried about disappointing the team I'd built and leaving behind people I loved.

As I sang, I closed my eyes, just trying to be present. That's when, in the middle of the music and my swirling thoughts, I saw a vision from God. I saw my own heart, like a house with every room carefully kept, places I'd worked so hard to tend and protect. Jesus was there, walking through each room, and there was such love in His eyes as He saw how I'd taken care to keep my heart pure.

But then He went to the back of my heart; a part I'd tried not to think about. There was a closet, boarded up tight with planks I'd nailed in myself after enough pain and disappointment. Jesus, gentle and patient, began to pry each board away. He didn't tear them off;

He honored the space and my story, gently removing what I had used to guard myself.

When He opened the closet door, the space was dark and heavy, but His love shone in...soft, real, and steady. Part of me wanted to hide, but there was also a quiet relief, like letting fresh air into a room that hadn't seen light for years. Jesus reached into the shadows, clearing away old cobwebs and lifting out a beautiful treasure box from behind dusty clothes.

The moment I saw that box, I felt a fresh wave of sorrow. I knew what was inside: all the dreams, promises, even the calling I'd wrapped up and buried behind discouragement and delay. The weight of those lost hopes settled over me. But Jesus stayed, love filling the room.

I watched Him pull out a golden key, delicate and bright. When He unlocked the treasure box, the whole space was flooded with light. It felt like hope coming back to life. Grief and disappointment melted away, replaced by the peace and joy only His presence brings.

When the vision ended, I knew it was time. Time to dust off what I'd hidden, to bring my dreams and God's Call on my life back out into the light. No more locking them away, no more living with my heart sectioned off.

It was time to say yes again, trusting that His love would be enough for every step ahead.

But saying yes didn't suddenly make everything clear or easy. The moment I committed to step forward, I found myself standing on unfamiliar ground - a holy invitation, but also a place of uncertainty.

It's the sacred place of being in the middle of transition.

There's a sacred phase in childbirth called "transition." It's that incredible threshold when a mother feels she has nothing left to give. When exhaustion and doubt peak, and the familiar comfort of control slips away. Yet, paradoxically, it's also the moment just before birth, the last surge of intensity right before new life arrives.

Having experienced the beauty and power of natural home births with both of my children, I learned firsthand what transition truly asks of us. It's not about pushing harder or tuning in to the energy of those around you. In fact, what transition demands is the opposite: a deeper letting go, an invitation to surrender.

During labor, real progress happens when we soften...when we yield to the process, trust the wisdom of our bodies, and allow the experience to unfold. Surrender isn't easy; it asks us to unclench our grip, to ease into discomfort, and to trust the arrival of something greater on the other side.

I believe this lesson reaches far beyond birth. Transition is a universal experience—a crossroads in life, in growth, in dreams coming to fruition. So often, our first instinct is to power through, to force or control outcomes. But again and again, we find that transformation calls us not into more striving, but into deeper trust. The courage to surrender, to soften instead of brace, is often what births the next chapter of our lives.

In life, there's a secret agony in transition that few talk about. The in-between is more than a waiting room. The middle. The letting go of the monkey bars and free-falling. It's a wilderness...a gap between the old and the new, the known and the unknown. It's where you feel the grief of what's ending, the fear of what's next, the restlessness of not yet arriving. You look around and see others stepping into their "promised land," while you're still in the field, still in the gap, still holding on for dear life as you let go of the monkey bars. You wonder if you missed your moment, if God has forgotten your address, if maybe you're just not meant for more.

But the ache you feel is holy. It's God's invitation to wake up to what's missing or to what has been hidden—the voice dimmed, the calling ignored, the fire you forced small so others wouldn't feel its heat.

I tried to silence it with busyness, with achievement, with anything that would keep me from feeling the discomfort of the in-between. But the ache was relentless. It was God's way of waking me up to the parts of myself I had buried, the dreams I had shelved, the calling I had tried to make more "palatable" for public consumption.

If you're feeling the ache, please don't ignore it. Don't rush past it. Let it lead you deeper. Let it show you where you've settled, where you've shrunk, where you've traded authenticity for acceptance. The ache is not your enemy. It's your invitation to break out of the box and Rise.

Boxes are sneaky. They start as boundaries: good intentions meant to keep us safe. But over time, they become prisons. We outgrow them, but we stay inside because it's familiar, because it's comfortable, because it's what people expect. My box was built with the bricks of other people's opinions. I let my brand become a cage, one that kept my faith quiet, my message muted, my calling confined to what was "acceptable." I told myself it was strategic, but really, it was survival.

What's your box made of? Is it the need for approval? The fear of rejection? The desire to be liked, even if it means being less than who you *really* are? Identifying your box is painful, but it's also powerful. It's the first step to breaking free. You can't rise if you're still trying to fit in the box you've outgrown.

But noticing the shape of your box is only the beginning. Real change comes when you dare to release it—when you're willing to step beyond the safety of what's familiar, even if every part of you wants to grip tighter. Growth begins the moment awareness is joined by surrender. That's where true freedom lives.

As you rise, know that surrender is the moment the monkey bars become real again. It's the moment you realize you can't keep holding on to what's safe and familiar and still move forward. It's when you realize more effort and performance isn't the answer. It's actually surrender. And surrender isn't passive. It's the bravest act of trust. It's releasing your grip of control and surrendering to the belief that God's arms are strong enough to catch you.

For me, surrender looked like letting go of the business I had built, the reputation I had protected, the version of myself that felt safe but suffocating. It looked like saying yes to the message God had placed on my heart, even when it didn't fit the mold, even when it meant losing opportunities, even when it meant being misunderstood, or could even offend others. Surrender is terrifying. It feels like free fall. But it's also the only way to truly rise. Sometimes the bravest thing you'll ever do is let go before you see the net, trusting that you will be caught.

As you let go and Rise, know that on the other side of surrender is space. At first it's the fear of the free fall, but then it's space to breathe, to speak, to live unboxed.

Rising is not about white-knuckling your way through life, nor is it about clinging tighter to things that quietly drain your spirit. True rising is found in the brave release–the moving forward, even as your heart trembles, guided by a whisper that you are meant for more.

It's learning to rise, even when fear shouts, even when others question, even as you mourn what you're asked to leave behind. Rising asks you to honor the ache and respond to the sacred invitation to become all you were created to be.

Throughout different major transitions of my life, I've come up with an acronym, and I hope it helps you recognize when it's your time to Rise.

The RISE Acronym

R — Recognize the Divine Discontentment

The ache of divine discontentment within is sacred - a holy restlessness that begins as a flicker and grows into a blazing call. It is the voice of God nudging you awake, stirring the embers of forgotten dreams and silent longings. This ache is not your enemy; it's the crossroads between comfort and calling. Don't quiet it down. Don't run from it. Be still. Let its ache guide you from the life you've settled for toward the life you were born to live.

"The ache you feel is not absence, but an invitation."

I — Identify the Box

Where have you built walls that now feel confining? Perhaps it's a job, a relationship, an identity, or a belief that keeps you dimmed. For me, it was a business that couldn't hold the wildfire of my bold faith. It was a script that felt safe while silencing my soul. Naming your box is the courage to see it. And when you see the box, you become free to outgrow it.

"You can't rise until you see the shape of what's been holding you down."

S — Surrender the Outcome

Surrender is not weakness. It's fearless trust in what you cannot yet see. In the Bible, we call it "faith," and in the Kingdom of God, faith is spelled "risk." It is that childhood moment on the playground: letting go of one bar before your hand finds the next or even letting go (like I did) and trusting that you will be caught by the loving arms of a good God. Surrender means releasing control and believing the ground beneath will appear, even when you're mid-air. Sometimes, the bravest act is letting go before the safety net is visible.

"Transformation always begins at the edge of letting go."

E — Embrace the Expansion

On the other side of surrender is sacred space–a breath of freedom and possibility. This is your unboxed life: where your voice is loud, your purpose is clear, and your story aligns with a higher plan. The dictionary describes alignment as "the correct position or positioning of components relative to one another so that they perform properly." When things are aligned, they are in the right position and place. When they are misaligned, something is out of place. When you surrender to the more of where you're being called to go and into who you're called to be, you step into greater alignment and expansion. Expansion is not just more; it's the right more. It's the moment your soul exclaims, *"Finally, I am home."*

"You rise the minute you refuse to shrink."

LET *your divine discontentment and call to rise awaken you. Name the box. Release the outcome. Receive the wide-open space that's calling you upward.*

The rise is waiting—will you say yes?

As you say yes, this is where alignment happens.

Your voice, your calling, and God's purpose finally fit together. Embracing the expansion means saying yes to the new, even when it's unfamiliar. It means letting God stretch you, grow you, and use you in ways you never imagined. It means living with open hands, trusting that what He has for you is better than anything you could build on your own. Expansion is uncomfortable. It requires faith. It requires courage. But it's also where you find your true voice, your true calling, your true self. Your rise begins the moment you stop shrinking.

Calling will cost you. But it's what you were made for.

There's a moment, sometimes right after we say yes to the more, when God invites us to trust Him again– not just with the big steps, but with the little choices that reveal where our faith truly lives. Sometimes it's the simplest moments that become the clearest mirrors of what we believe about worth, surrender, and the cost of what really matters.

When my son was little, he was obsessed with Thomas the Tank Engine from "Thomas & Friends." For his birthday, I went shopping, scanning the shelves for a gift. I found a little train toy in the discount section: affordable, easy, disposable. But then, I felt a nudge from God: "Get the real Thomas. The one that costs more." I argued with God in my head. My son was in a phase where every toy was picked up and dropped, picked up and dropped, until it broke. Why spend more on something that would just end up in pieces? But the nudge persisted. So I bought the more expensive Thomas the Tank Engine.

True to form, my son was thrilled. He picked up the train, dropped it. Picked it up, dropped it. Over and over, day after day.

Two weeks went by....Pick up, drop.

Four weeks...Pick up, drop.

Months passed, and still, that little train kept rolling. It was battered and scratched, but it never broke and it still had its little "choo-choo."

A year later, when my son finally outgrew Thomas, we took it to the donation center. He smiled at me, picked it up, and dropped it one more time for old time's sake. The train was worn, but still *choo-chooing* its way into the donation bin.

Watching it disappear, I thought about the manufacturer, the designer who knew a little boy would play rough, who built that toy to withstand the banging. Then I thought about us. About how our Creator, in the assembly line of life, knew exactly what we would face. He knew we'd be picked up, dropped, betrayed, and banged up through life. But He didn't create us to fall apart and break.

You were created for the Call on your life. You were made to last. Your calling will cost you, yes. You'll be picked up and dropped, misunderstood and misused, battered and bruised. But you were built for this.

You were made to withstand the journey. The scratches and dents are not signs of failure, they're proof that you've been used for your purpose.

Lasting things are made with intention for the journey, not just for show. Our purpose, like that train, was never about staying pristine or untouched. We're meant for the kind of living that leaves marks...sometimes battered, sometimes misunderstood, but always moving forward

---

That moment reminded me: the cost of stepping into your calling isn't measured by what you can hold on to, but by what you're willing to let go and the cost you're willing to pay for your Calling.

Our Creator designed us with resilience for the bumps, the letting go, the new beginnings. It challenges us to trust that being "used up" in service of something eternal is far more beautiful than appearing flawless on the surface.

So yes, letting go of what looks successful on the outside, but stifles your soul, is painful. I know. I mourned the loss of influence, relationships, and the image of who I thought I needed to be. Yet, just like that sturdy train, what remains after surrender is what truly lasts. God met me in the in-between, setting my voice free, inviting me to live the story He's been writing all along.

There's still fear, still the sting of misunderstanding, but there's also peace–a deep, quiet assurance that God is present in the hardest transitions, unraveling old lies, redeeming what feels lost, and beckoning you to step into your calling without clinging to what was.

The in-between isn't a detour or a failure. It's where God crafts the most essential things in us: identity, a firm foundation, courage, trust, and authenticity. It's where He clears away the unnecessary, so He can fill us with what endures. And it's here, if we listen, that we begin to recognize His voice even when nothing looks certain, and take hold of the life we were truly made to live.

I think of Peter, stepping out of the boat with eyes fixed on Jesus. The wind howling, waves crashing, but the invitation from Jesus was clear: "Come." Nothing in his circumstances looked like stepping out of the boat and walking on water was possible. I mean, who here thinks they can walk on water?! But when Peter got out of the boat and trusted Jesus called him, he did the impossible. How radically *wild* and *bold!* (This story can be found in Matthew 14:22-33).

Rising looks like risk. Like obedience in uncertainty. Like trusting Jesus is enough, even when you're not sure you are. And especially when everything around you looks like it's impossible.

Another thing to understand is that rising doesn't require more effort, performance, or to hustle harder. It requires rest and surrender.

Think of the story of Mary and Martha. Martha was doing good things. Lots of them. Hustling and bustling around all the while, Mary was sitting at Jesus' feet, choosing presence over performance. Rising looks like rest. Like choosing what matters most, even when the world is busy with lesser things. (This story can be found in Luke 10:38-42).

Think of Jesus, kneeling in the garden, sweating blood as He surrendered His will to the Father. Everything in who He was as a man was filled with anxiety, so much so that he sweated blood. And everything in Him being fully God, surrendered to the call on His life and the will of God, because there was a bigger purpose at play. (This story can be found in Luke 22).

Rising looks like surrender. Like trusting resurrection is coming, even when all you see is the cross.

Whether you're a Christ-follower or not, the ancient stories told in the Bible contain examples of radical risk and completely supernatural things, that it wrecks me for anything but an ordinary, mundane life.

Their rise began with letting go. So will yours. So has mine.

Let's be honest: just like the stories in the bible, we know that the in-between is not comfortable. It's the place where your faith is tested, where your motives are refined, where your identity is stripped down to its core. It's the place where God asks you to trust Him with your reputation, your relationships, and your future. You'll feel the pull of the old, the lure of the familiar, the temptation to go back to what's safe. You'll hear voices - internal and external - telling you to stay in the box, to settle for what's good instead of reaching for what's God. But you'll also feel the invitation - the gentle, persistent tug of the Spirit calling you forward, calling you higher, calling you deeper.

The in-between is where you learn to trust the process, to honor the journey, to believe that God is at work even when you can't see the results. Rising isn't about climbing higher. It's about surrendering deeper. It's not about proving, but about abiding. Being. It's not about being understood, but about being faithful. God is not looking for perfection. He's looking for your yes. He's looking for hearts that are willing to say yes, even when the cost is high. He's looking for voices that are willing to speak, even when the room is silent. He's looking for the willingness of a little boy to bring his 5 loaves and 2 fish to miraculously feed a multitude (see Matthew 14:13-21). He's looking for you to bring what little you have in your hand so He can do what only He can do. He's looking for lives that are willing to be poured out, even when the world doesn't understand.

If you are reading this and don't know Jesus but something in your spirit is longing to know Him... even now as you're reading this, I believe the Spirit of the living God is going to encounter you in a powerful way. You may be feeling heat, or deep peace that you haven't felt in a long time... maybe your eyes are tearing up or something in your "knowing" is longing for Him...however you are encountering Him now, know that you're being pursued and called by the Creator of the universe and it's time to invite Him to be the Lord of your life...or maybe you know Him but somewhere along your journey, you've drifted away and you're ready to recommit your life to living for His plan... Either way, you're ready to allow Him to lead you into the most beautiful Spirit-filled adventure that will unlock your divine destiny, then pray this prayer:

"JESUS, *I believe in you and that you are the Son of God. Forgive me for the places where I have clung to control, where I've missed the mark, sinned, and tried to make a god out of everything else but you. Thank you for the gift of your grace and for dying on the cross for me—something I could never earn or perform for...it was something you did because you loved me and thought I was worth it, even in the middle of my mess. Come into my heart, clear away the cob webs, let your love and Spirit fill me. Ignite my God-given identity and destiny and guide me on a journey with you that I never could have imagined. Teach me to know your heart, to trust your ways, to walk by faith, and help bring heaven to earth. In Jesus' name I pray, Amen.*"

IF YOU PRAYED this prayer and meant it, the Bible says that all of heaven rejoices, and my friend, I am celebrating too! Being a follower of Jesus is the most incredible decision you could ever make.

Did you know that Jesus fulfilled over 300 Old Testament prophecies? That's not luck. That's divine design. Statistically, the chance of fulfilling just 8 of these is 1 in 100 quadrillion (this is 1,000,000,000,000,000. That's 15 zeros after it, and Jesus fulfilled *hundreds* of prophecies!)

The Bible isn't just a collection of stories. It's a connected story that points straight to Jesus.

He didn't come to fit in. He came to fulfill it all. And He is alive and more real than I could ever explain.

I've seen miracles, healings, signs, and wonders that blow every box of my safe world out of the water.

I've prayed for people who were in pain, and they've immediately felt no pain.

I've seen gold dust appear on my hands and the hands of others because the Spirit of God was so manifest in a room.

God has given me prophetic words over the lives and over the future of others that only Heaven would have known.

He is not a powerless, distant, far-off God, and the Bible is not a powerless Gospel. It is *good news!* He is closer than your breath and promises to never abandon or leave you. He is not the universe. He is the creator of the universe - every universe. His game plan and timeline are relationship, forever, and we were created for it. As Sons and Daughters of God, we don't live *for* love, we live *from* love.

There's nothing we could do for Him that would make Him love us any more or any less because He, in and of Himself, IS love. His commission is for us to know Him and make earth more like heaven, where we walk in communion with Him and with each other, where there is no pain, no sickness, no disasters or darkness. I could go on and on and on...

If this is new to you, I highly encourage you to start to learn about Jesus and read the Bible with an open heart. Start in the New Testament and know that the Old Testament all point to Jesus. There's a great YouTube channel called "The Bible Project," and my favorite reading plan is called "The Bible Recap," which will help you understand more cultural contexts and some of the mysteries and language that can be found in the ancient text.

And if you want to grow in knowing more of your identity, I invite you to grab a copy of my prophetic devotional called *"The Pathway to the Heart of the Father."* It can be found on Amazon and is a beautiful devotional that is igniting an army of fiery revivalists who are walking boldly in their God given identity and calling.

Now, to be vulnerable, even as I write this, if this is making you feel uncomfortable, it's not meant to. I'm hoping you won't be offended that I'm boldly sharing my faith. Know that if it's not for you, that's ok. I still love you, accept you exactly where you are, even if we have different beliefs, and honor you as the amazing human that you are. I know this may feel uncomfortable, and that's ok too. Even for me, this invitation in a very public manner feels risky to my tender heart, and all of the fears I wrote about are screaming in my mind to *delete, delete delete*...

But I can't not...

Not anymore...

And whether or not we believe the same thing, I hope that even this very real-time example has given you permission to do the same in whatever area this applies to you.

Before I conclude this chapter, I want to honor the remarkable women contributing to this book, each bringing her own unique perspective. Some share my beliefs, while others see things differently. The boldness and conviction in my chapter reflect my story alone and aren't meant to speak for anyone else's.

We each carry enough strength and wisdom to understand that there's space for every woman to rise, courageous and true to her own beliefs within her unique journey, without choosing offense when those beliefs don't align. Offense is a choice, but so is respect. Here, we're committed to honoring one another and rising together. On this journey, we don't demand everyone think the same; we seek unity, not uniformity. True unity means coming together and valuing one another, differences and all. I truly believe the rising of women, in its fullest sense, will only happen when more of us embrace this truth–when we choose honor, respect, and collective strength over division.

A Holy Charge to Rise

As this chapter closes, I want to leave you with more than inspiration...I want to leave you with a holy summons.

There is an ache inside you...the quiet longing for more, the hunger to live truly free. That divine discontentment is not your enemy; it's God's invitation. The tension you feel in the in-between, the unrest of transition, the quiet fear as you stand on the edge - these are holy ground. You're not lost; you're being called.

I charge you: let the ache wake you up. Let the box you've outgrown become the doorway, not your prison. Surrender the need to have it all figured out, to stay in what's familiar, or to be accepted by those who never saw the fire in you to begin with. Step into the discomfort of the unknown because it's there that you will meet God, not as the memory of yesterday, but as the builder of your tomorrow.

On the other side of surrender is space, sweet space for your soul to expand with courage, for your voice to rise unmuted, for your purpose to align with heaven's heartbeat. You were not created to shrink. You were built to withstand the banging, the drop, the uncertainty - to be used for every ounce of purpose God infused into you.

Ask yourself now: *Where do you feel the holy ache of transition?*

What box have you stayed in too long? What outcome is God inviting you to surrender, and where is He nudging you toward wild expansion? Write it down. Pray it through. Listen for His whisper.

The wilderness is not a waste; it's preparation. You're not being punished in the in-between. You're being prepared, forged, and commissioned.

Sometimes the bravest thing you'll ever do is let go before you see the net. Trust that the same God who called you is already in your next chapter, already making rivers in your wasteland.

May you be filled with outrageous courage. May fear be overshadowed by expectancy. May you rise, not in striving, but in surrender. May your voice be heard, not because it's perfect, but because it's willing and yielded.

Let the divine discontentment move you. Lean into the stretch. Let go before you see the net, and believe that what God has for you on the other side is more than your best effort could ever build. Don't shrink. Don't play safe. You were made for the holy in-between, made to move, made for the wild possibility of God. Meant for More.

This is your time. No more shrinking, no more playing small. The world needs your voice - not polished, but present; not perfect, but *brave*. Even if it still shakes. I'm cheering you on, step by messy step, from my own set of monkey bars.

You are braver than you know. The middle is holy ground. God's not done with your story; He's just getting started.

So, dear friend, rise. The world needs the fullness of who you really are. Your story, your surrender, your rising - it's not just for you. It's an anthem of hope, a declaration that the middle really is where miracles are born. And that you *are Meant For More...*

With you in every step,

Charity

"See, I am doing a new thing! Now it springs up; do you not perceive it? I am making a way in the wilderness and streams in the wasteland." — Isaiah 43:19

If you're standing at your own set of monkey bars, hands aching, heart pounding - *come with me. The Brave in the Between Guidebook* is your invitation to let go and discover the arms that are waiting to catch you.

Get your copy of the Brave in the Between Guidebook: a companion for every sacred transition by going to WeAreMeantForMore.com/brave-guidebook.

And if you're hungry for even more breakthrough, my book *Meant for More: Igniting Your Purpose in a World that Tries to Dim Your Light* is available now on Amazon. It's the story of what happens when you refuse to settle, when you trust God with your journey, and when you discover that the middle is where miracles are born.

Let's keep connecting. Find resources, encouragement, and community at <u>CharityMajors.com</u> and WeAreMeantForMore.com

Connect with me @CharityMajors on Instagram.

You're not alone in this. I'm cheering you on, every step of the way. We've got this!

———

Charity Majors

Charity Majors is a dynamic author, prophetic voice, and sought-after speaker with a passion for igniting purpose in hearts that feel called to more. As the founder of Meant For More Ministries, Charity is devoted to helping women and leaders everywhere break free from the boxes of limitation, rise above the noise of comparison, and discover a life aligned with their God-given identity and calling.

With a background spanning personal growth, business leadership, spiritual mentorship, and building empowering communities and cultures. Charity brings wisdom shaped by overcoming adversity, deep faith, and authentic connection. Her ministry is a movement for those who feel the holy ache for more, guiding individuals from striving and self-doubt to surrender, purpose, power and true spiritual expansion.

Charity's bestselling book, "Meant for More: Igniting Your Purpose in a World That Tries to Dim Your Light," is a beacon for those ready to move from playing small to living boldly and unapologetically in their calling. Her prophetic devotional, "Pathway to the Heart of the Father," offers daily encouragement for drawing nearer to God, tuning in to His voice, and navigating the brave steps of faith required to pursue your unique path. Her other books include "Their Ceiling, Your Floor," and "Connection Capital" along with her podcast called 'Meant For More."

Known for her heartfelt storytelling and practical yet powerful teaching, Charity empowers others to recognize the ache for more as a divine invitation. She believes transformation doesn't come through striving, but through yielded courage, faith, and an open heart— a message woven through every facet of her work.

Whether leading retreats, teaching workshops, or sharing on stage, Charity is committed to creating space where voices are set free, dreams are dusted off, and every person realizes they were made for a purpose far greater than what the world has to offer.

Charity resides with her husband and children, cherishing family, adventure, and the unexpected journey of walking out God's promises. Through every lesson, she invites you to trust, and remember: you *are* Meant for More.

To connect with Charity, find resources, or invite her to speak or minister, visit **CharityMajors.com.**

It's easy, after so many pages, to close a book and move on...to let the stories settle as gentle inspiration before daily life drowns them out. But let this be your invitation not to let these stories be the end, but the beginning.

THE WOMEN in these pages are proof that rising isn't reserved for someone else, in another time, with a different past. Their stories are not distant echoes. They are sparks meant to light the fire within *you*.

You have felt the shiver of recognition in these words: the ache of a familiar struggle, the jolt of a shared hope. Don't let that connection fade. *This is your dawn.*

If you have ever doubted your voice, questioned your place, or hesitated at the threshold of your own power, know this: *now* is *your time* to *rise.*

These stories are permission slips, yes...but they are also *challenges*: will you carry the lessons forward? Will you let these women's courage wake your own, let their wisdom become your compass? Will you step out of the shadows of hesitation and into the steady glow of your own rising?

The story of rise is not complete without you.

We want to hear your voice, honor your courage, and add your journey to the tapestry that gives us all strength. Your scars and triumphs, your questions and your clarity - they belong here, with all of us.

So don't keep your story hidden. Share it—boldly, messily, beautifully. The world needs what you carry and there are people waiting to hear the wisdom you have within.

Go to the link below, and tell us your Rise story. Let the world feel the ripple of your ascent. Let your journey be the light that calls another woman to step bravely forward.

The next page is empty, waiting for your words. Because together, our stories don't just connect us... they change us.

And when you rise, you help us all to rise.

Now, it's *your* turn.

Share your RISE by going to this link: https://bit.ly/share-my-rise